Shamanism

Know More About the Practices of Shamanism

(Reconnecting Heaven & Earth Through the Art of Shamanism)

Marlon Swink

Published By **John Kembrey**

Marlon Swink

All Rights Reserved

Shamanism: Know More About the Practices of Shamanism (Reconnecting Heaven & Earth Through the Art of Shamanism)

ISBN 978-1-77485-569-0

No part of this guidebook shall be reproduced in any form without permission in writing from the publisher except in the case of brief quotations embodied in critical articles or reviews.

Legal & Disclaimer

The information contained in this ebook is not designed to replace or take the place of any form of medicine or professional medical advice. The information in this ebook has been provided for educational & entertainment purposes only.

The information contained in this book has been compiled from sources deemed reliable, and it is accurate to the best of the Author's knowledge; however, the Author cannot guarantee its accuracy and validity and cannot be held liable for any errors or omissions. Changes are periodically made to this book. You must consult your doctor or get professional medical advice before using any of the suggested remedies, techniques, or information in this book.

Upon using the information contained in this book, you agree to hold harmless the Author from and against any damages, costs, and expenses, including any legal fees potentially resulting from the application of any of the information provided by this guide. This disclaimer applies to any damages or injury caused by the use and application, whether directly or indirectly, of any advice or information presented, whether for breach of contract, tort, negligence, personal injury, criminal intent, or under any other cause of action.

You agree to accept all risks of using the information presented inside this book. You need to consult a professional medical practitioner in order to ensure you are both able and healthy enough to participate in this program.

TABLE OF CONTENTS

Introduction 1

Chapter 1: The Origins Of Shamanism 5

Chapter 2: Reclaiming The Soul 32

Chapter 3: Guided Imagery 41

Chapter 4: Role Of The Shaman 77

Chapter 5: Shamanism Beliefs 80

Chapter 6: What Shamanism Believes Have To Do With Spirit And Soul Concepts 82

Chapter 7: The Tools Used In Shamanism 91

Chapter 8: Relationship To The Pachamama 100

Chapter 9: Shamanic Skills 121

Chapter 10: Shamanic Journeying 142

Chapter 11: Work With Plants 167

Conclusion 183

Introduction

Shamanism is a long-standing spiritual faith that is a part of people of the Turkic and Mongolian people's who reside throughout Siberia, Central Asia and in the western regions in Eastern Europe. It is a popular belief in Mongolia and Siberia it is often referred to as "Tengerism" because it refers to "honoring the spirits".

Shamanism is not a religious practice, it's actually a technique. It is a practice that coexists with a variety of existing religions in different cultures. In Siberia it is possible to find shamanism , which is a part of Lamaism and Buddhism and, in the nation of Japan It is also a part of Buddhism.

There is no doubt that a large number of shamans reside in animistic religions and animism implies that people believe in the existence of spirits. It is equally crucial to be aware that Shamanism is not an exclusive or an esoteric system of belief.

The Basics

Shamanism was first observed by Western observers

living in v in s herding societies across central and northern Asia . It is from the language spoken by one of these societies the Tungus-speaking Siberia-speaking peoples which the word "shaman" came to be developed.

This word comes from "saman" from the Siberian Tungustic which means "one who is excited, raised and moved" and can also be used to describe people who, in state of trance travel to the realm of many supernatural beings to communicate with and interact with them. During the process, gain the power of the mystical. Thus, in the language of Tungus shaman is someone who is on an excursion into the unordinary reality.

The main function of shamans who practice this technique, also known as shamanism is to assist the dead in their journey to the afterlife. The Shaman is the mediator between the living and the dead.

They also determine the appropriate type of medicine to treat

their patients from their patients from m a their patients from the mystical beings. In

Certain areas, Shamanism does not really require a power to heal or treat a specific disease, but also identify the root of the problem

or malady.

A lot of people, particularly today, aren't sure the meaning of shamanism. There are numerous words like sorcerer, witch doctor as well as wizards that each have different meanings, preconceptions, and meanings that are connected to these terms. While the term "shaman" originates from Siberia the technique or practice of Shamanism is found on many continents.

The majority of the time, Shamans are also referred as "people who have knowledge" as seers, in the context of their native tribes because they participate in an established system of knowledge that is based upon firsthand experiences. It is crucial to realize that Shamanism isn't really an ideology of belief.

It's actually based on certain personal studies that are carried out to gather information, heal, and many other things. In actual If these shamans are not able to achieve results, then they'll not be able to be utilized by their community. If you're wondering what you can do to tell whether someone is an shaman, it's extremely simple. They can do magic and travel into the realms of the other. It is an approach to live living that allows you to become one with all creation as well as the natural world.

Chapter 1: The Origins Of Shamanism

What is Shaman? Shaman?

We'll begin by trying to describe what we are referring to by Shaman. In order to do this, we need to take a look at these communities that existed and have been around for hundreds of years in different areas of the world. Within many of them communities, we can see the image of Shaman. Shaman.

As per Olga Roig, "The Shaman is the wizard from the clan, and more than all, he's an individual with the power of". It is said that the Shaman doesn't have any magic skills, nor is he a or a diviner, healer, or doctors, nor is he priest. He blends all of these professions and Western classifications into one subject who holds the power. The ability to communicate with the Gods and spirits and archetypes, to see the visible and the invisible. isn't.

From a analytical perspective scientists in the science of Anthropology identify Shaman from a more scientific perspective. Shaman in terms of "an interlocutors between the spiritual and the natural worlds".

What is the source of the Shamanism worldview come from?

Studies accepted by historians reveal that the origins of what we call "Shamanism" is situated in Siberia. Scientists such as ethno-semiotics often believe that Shamanic roots to petroglyphs and stones-engraved figures that are believed to date in the 9000-7000 years B.C. located in the eastern region of Siberia.

There is evidence to suggest that practices, which appear similar to Siberian Shamanism, took place across various geographic regions in a way that was spontaneously.

Amerindian of Latin America or Shamanism

While Shamanism is rooted in Siberia in the above paragraphs but over time, it has expanded to different regions of the globe. In this instance, to go further into Shamanism within Latin America or also called Amerindian Shamanism, as we discover their beliefs and practices quite interesting.

When we speak of Amerindian or Latin American Shamanism, we mean the shamanic practices used -and continue to be being practiced in the various warrior and hunting ethnic groups across Latin America: such as the ones from Colombia, Peru, Bolivia, Argentina, Ecuador, Mexico, Brazil, Guatemala, Dominican Republic, Paraguay, Venezuela, etc.

Every tribe or ethnic group of Latin America is unique; and , as such, has distinct characteristics that make it unique.

So, even though this practice has similarities in characteristics and rituals as other shamanic practices around the world, they are distinct from the other. Every shaman has specific rituals that are specific to the environment that they reside in and to the natural resources available within the region.

There are Shamanic ethnicities across all countries that make up the vast area that is Latin America. Additionally every country has a variety of different ethnic communities within them. For instance, within Ecuador The "Taromenane" are situated at the border of Ecuador and Peru and are considered to be an important cultural and human treasure. The "Tagaeri" are also part of their own Ecuadorian jungle. "Tsachila" is the name of the tribe "Tsachila" is located within the county of Santo Domingo de los Colorados.

Within the nation of "Tsachila" There are communities that include the Chihuilpe and the Congoma and the Bua The Naranjos The Poste The Peripa and the Tahuasa as well as Otonco Mapali. Otonco Mapali. Within the Ecuadorian Amazon are the "Shuar".

In the same way that we discuss the diversity of ethnic groups in Ecuador and the surrounding countries, we can continue to mention the diverse ethnic groups that reside in each country of Latin America.

As one would expect as is to be expected, the image of the Shaman will come with different denominations according to the tribe we belong to. Mircea Eliade explains that each Shaman will have a distinct denomination based on the place of their birth and, more specifically, in accordance with the tribe they are a part of. Within people belonging to the Guaimi Indians the Chaman will be referred to as "krokodianga" while for those of the Choco Indians it will be named "Jaybana okura bana"; "Page" across several South American tribes; "machi" in the West Coast of South America; "Piache" on the Amazon River; "Angakok" between the Esqui and Kone" in the Land of Fire. (Eliade, 1960)

The problem that pops up here is:

How can we talk about "Shamanism" in general when there are so many different ethnic groups practicing various things using different languages and various names?

To be able to answer this question to answer this question, we will need to look into the existence of something that binds all practices that are common to all ethnic groups that is, something that is essential enough to allow them to be put together. We will seek to discover, that which is Essence of Shamanism.

Shamanism and its Essence of Shamanism

If one is required to define in a general way, exactly what's the most fundamental element that is at the heart or the fundamental essentials of Shamanism? It is our opinion that it is a good idea for us to be following Josep Fericgla who believes that the most important part of shamanic practice:

"The process of connecting - without any effortin a non-confrontational way with the hidden dimensions of reality by way of techniques that alter the state of consciousness that is normal [...]" (Fericgla 2000).).

This will be a breakdown of the definition to allow us to understand its full meaning more carefully.

The process of making "contact" with unobserved entities is truly amazing. It is an utter break that plays out of the melody of academic logic which is the logic of science and its methodology. If we are to judge based on rationality the idea of contact with Unseen entities would appear to be a part of a fantasy, a fallacious and untrue story. yet it is more compelling than the experience of that first contact.

On the contrary, when the author talks about the secret dimension of the world, he is referring to the relationship to Shaman Shaman as well as Gods of Nature. Natural Gods, that is in between the Shaman and his fellow Forces of Nature.

The third reason is that when the author refers to the normal state, he is referring to the everyday state of consciousness. This is, a normal state of consciousness that was not, up until that point altered by a psychoactive substance.

Furthermore, we will clarify that when he refers to Techniques for altering the regular state of consciousness, he refers to techniques that alter the everyday state of consciousness, which is, methods that permit the transition from the everyday state into a completely different state that we refer to as an altered state of mind.

The most common method of achieving the ecstasy state is to consume psychoactive substances that come that are derived from plants that are native to each area.

When the author talks about psychoactive substances, they refer to substances that alter the physiological state of our state of consciousness. For instance, these are substances that we use every day and are all around us such as caffeine, alcohol cigarettes, alcohol, drugs and so on.

There are some compounds that we do not know about yet, however they are the ones that Shamans from Latin America usually use, which also have a psychoactive effect like peyote, Ayahuasca, San Pedro cactus cebil, mezcal salvia, belladonna, datura cannabis.

They can also turn to altered states in response to drum percussion such as fasting, vigils, methods of sensory deprivation, sweating hutsand sweating.

These techniques create changes to the regular condition of mind of Shamans.

In this altered state the people will be able to rise and begin the Shamanic trance.

The author who mentioned Joseph Fericgla-delved deeper into his descriptions and gives us a detailed description of the moment in the trance that is very interesting. The author explains that:

"The Shaman keeps his consciousness active in both realities. [...] In this manner, He actively seeks out ghosts or other characters that reside in his subconscious to try to organize them in accordance with his own interests and those of his group". (Fericgla, 2000).

The balance of consciousness between two dimensions, or planes of reality is of paramount significance. In this way the concept that the Shaman as an intermediary between the physical and spiritual worlds is sketched.

On contrary it's fascinating and natural that the Shaman's love for the community should be apparent. Because, it's to this community that he is a part of and it's also to the members of that community that he has entrusted the future of his decisions.

Awakening of Consciousness

Spiritual absence

Nowadays, we reside in urban areas that shift closer and further away from the natural essence of Human. Modern urban life, which is modern and everyday, hides nature from us, and gives us a new set of priorities. There are endless entertainment options such as videogames, series Whatsapp, Instagram, Facebook and more. The rationale of consumption and money continues to guide our choices in our actions, our schedules and priorities. The speed and pace of cities in the major cities, the transportation cut as well as the time to travel require us to be a bit more efficient and make us tired.

On the other hand, we are facing an era of decline for traditional religions. For the sake of science-based reasoning the traditional religions have long been scrutinized by people and have ceased to serve as spiritual references for a huge segment of the people.

This entire panorama hints at an issue of spiritual absence. A vacant spirituality. A spirituality that requires to be enriched with new perceptions and frameworks. A spirituality that requires to connect with more distant entities. A spirituality that requires new symbols and practices, as well as new codes.

Humans are social creatures that need to make Presence visible in the absence, and to create light in the darkness. In absence, we do not exist. In absence, there are no developments that could be possible There is no reproduction, there's no death at all. In the darkness it is impossible to see. It isn't possible to travel forever in it, nor be a food source for it. Additionally, the dark presents ever-changing challenges to us that we're not prepared to face.

It is not possible to simply choose to go about our lives and project ourselves onto an absence or darkness.

: SHAMANISM HEALING TECHNIQUES

Presentation

The book is a compilation of work-related exercises that the goal is to increase awareness of the world around us. The first section of this book is focused on essential sensory experiences and the final part is a trance state and stupor management and also a small portion of the basic gathering process necessary to assist others to enter them.

These methods don't create a shaman however, they draw from the shamanic view that is based on an increased focus on our surroundings and the ability to move between the ordinary and the sacred parts of our lives.

"Strolling between the Worlds" demands that we determine ways to enhance our knowledge of the traditional, in order to discover the extra standard that is present in the text. Many of the techniques need a bunch of investigation because it is hard to create without separating yourself from other people.

Shamans are spiritual creatures that have the ability to heal energy, harness energies as well as "see" visions. Shamans' primary characteristics include the dominance of vitality as well as fire as a tool for transformation.

Shamanism encompasses a variety of traditional beliefs and practices that have the ability to analyse remedies, heal, and again and again create human suffering through crossing the hub mundi and creating a unique relationship with, or taking control over spirits.

Shamans are believed to have the ability to control weather, divination, perception of dreaming, projection into the astral and flying into the both the lower and upper universes. Shamanistic traditions have been a part of the culture throughout the world since the earliest times.

Shamanism has its roots in the belief that the visible world is ruled by invisible powers or spirits that impact the lives of those who live. In contrast to animism and animatisms that are found in generally all people from are commonplace practices Shamanism demands a specific level of knowledge or abilities.

Shamans aren't or, as the case might, divided into full-time customs or profound relationships, like clergymen. Shamans assume the role of healer in the shamanic social order Shamans gather information and power by traversing the world of hubs and information from the heavens.

Even in the western world the old-fashioned practice of fixing is mentioned through the use by the caduceus to represent an symbol of medicine.

The shaman generally is able to access, or even secure at least one of the natural substances that aid in the realm of the soul They are typically spirits from the structure of creatures spirits of plants that heal as well as (here here and there) the spirits of left-handed shamans. In many shamanic orders magic, enchantment, power of the mystical as well as information are represented by one word, such as that of the Quechua expression.

The causes of illnesses are thought to lie within an area of the deep and arousing of vindictive spirits or Witchcraft as well as spiritual methods and as well as what we might call physical methods are used to recover. The shaman will naturally be in the body of their patient to locate the soul, making the patient wipe out, and then recover by removing the soul that is enticing from the patient.

However many shamans are masters in their knowledge of the plants within their immediate vicinity and a personal routine is often advised as a method of treatment. In numerous places, the shaman's intention is to profit from plants in particular is simply having the ability to assess the impact of a plant , and then use it to heal after getting to know the spirit of the plant, and receiving permission.

Certain social orders recognize those shamans who heal from alchemists that hurt. Others believe that all shamans possess the capacity to heal as well as murder. That is, shamans are part of some social orders thought to be able to heal harm.

The shaman often does doesn't appreciate the extraordinary power and glory within the community, well-known for their abilities and their knowledge but they could also be linked to hurting people and are thus feared.

Participating in this activity, the shaman exposes himself to significant risk to himself and danger from the spiritual realm as well as from any other shamans that are in conflict with him and also by the techniques used to change his state of consciousness.

The plant materials used can cause death and the experience of being out of body itself could trigger non-returning or physical death. The appearance of assurance are common and the use of dangerous plants is often deeply ritualized.

To harness the power that spirits have the world, shamans embark on an attempt to reach out to the spirit world. In the past, people performed music or sung in tune, and the sound was strong enough that shamans lost the normal feeling of being accessible to the world.

They could end up cruising in a different world that was not created by the shaman's ability to create due to the fact that, when the event happened to them and they were in another place. The access to this world is possible under the surface of the earth under the earth, submerged or frozen or even high up on a mountain or within the fogs.

The shaman might be a spirit or a soul from the past with information on recuperating, both of which are aids. During the course of an experience, the assistant can help the shaman guard the soul of the sufferer, and bring it back to its owner.

The majority of the shamanic system of control is more prominent than the typical physical forces we encounter in everyday life. There are also the forces that a shaman has: the hands-on power to heal by eliminating hurtful soul material from the body , or to restore the body's vitality, the ability to look through a dreamlike way the physical body of burned out person; and the capability to retrieve the soul that was lost by those who are weak.

Shamanism also offers a form of knowledge that is hard to describe, such as being in contact with other creatures or even help from the spirit of a creature. It provides the sensation of closeness of the progenitors of one's or well-disposed dead who offer assistance.

A shaman who is in fantasiac or on a soul journey might have a vision of future events; shamanism could provide insight into the location of lost objects or individuals, along with the ability to find these things.

Shamanism is a strange way to alter the atmosphere and give an individual a physical appearance that is difficult to comprehend and, in a curious way, show the power of bi-

area to appear in two places in a flash. It is always a source of people joy or makes them smile.

The best way to understand the shamanism phenomenon is to feel an underlying medium which everyone experiences that is a source of energy that goes beyond the normal, a type of medium which also creates a permeability between people to each the other. It is best understood through experiences from real life because of it being amongst more this force is difficult to define.

These stories illustrate the sense of connection the Inupiat provide soul-creatures and the power of meeting spirits. They're not just joking stories. What's the basis of cognizance which is cultivated in shamans when they heal?

When an Inupiat healer puts her fingers on the human body's aching tissue This is a display of genuine inter-dimensional connection with the other.

The person suffering from the condition is not able to feel the hand's weight. Nor will help occur due to the fact that the sufferer believes that something is going to occur.

What happens is which isn't even viewed but those who suffer from this condition understand that it is a real issue as it develops. It's a matter of relationships.

People are aware of their associations with each other. They constantly seek to strengthen their common associations in order to live. The human brain can "read" non-verbal communications We can also "read" love; however, when we recover, there is an additional cost that is a kind of supporter fee, that is passed with the hands of the healer.

The constant, universal closeness of being connected can transfer energy and strength from person to person, much like the air transports our voices. Through this connection, people are able to access the forces of the shaman. In many religions, there's an awareness of the spirit or force element that acts as a mediator and grants blessings (however every now and then is this kind of mindfulness present within the philosophical and academic parts of the world religions).

A soul that connects exists to connect people in a way that an shaman may be able to join with other people to help them heal. This soul the shaman might also be able to return after death to assist others and deliver clear messages when needed; and in the afterlife like holy persons and an angel or Delphic prophet, they may come to know the purposes that are visible throughout the entire, interconnected web.

Mindfulness and the fusion of these connections are more clearly seen in the various religious beliefs, as well as to the daily routine and experience of the social orders of the seeker-gatherer.

The shaman in this time of joy keeps the control of his body, and comes back with messages for recovering. The use of psychedelic drugs isn't considered to be a way of achieving enjoyment. "The joy of the shaman is different from the supernatural and prophetic happiness of the artists and the priests.

The shaman is not merely believe in the divine; he is an integral part of it, and part of the elements that comprise the various universes. Through this control, not the loss of control, that he is able reach higher levels of consciousness and communicate with spirits, into obscure and occult information, and to bring about non-obtrusive enhancements within the "otherworld" which will result in real physical effects on the world of "common reality".

Shamanic Cosmology

The shamanic cosmology consists of an upper and lower world as well as a central world and a lower. The center world connects to earth, while the lower and upper universes transcend space and time. The shaman journeys through the upper and lower universes in search of soul aids and force creatures who assist the shaman recuperate from work. Force creatures are associated within the realm of modeling reality.

They possess distinctive characteristics that differ from animals in that they may provide and could have unique characteristics. The purpose in the role of force creatures is safeguard us across all universes in order to provide direction and support and ensure wellbeing and prosperity.

Tree of Life connects the higher, middle and lower universes, and represents the vital stream that maintains life on the earth. This is why the shaman is a channel for healing and vital energy. It is essential to link the world of earth with the sacred objects that provide meaning and direction. The shaman's journey demonstrates the connection between the universes of infinite and teaches us that all things are alive and interconnected.

The journey of the shamans starts at the center of the universe, and she is looking for an open space in earth, such as hollows or a gap in the middle of the tree. She walks through a tunnel that is able to slide into the lower world and is able to experience a scene from a non-conventional realities, which could be the wood-land or seascape.

This is where she connects with her soulmates who help her find the direction she'll need to learn more and assist others. The adventure in the upper world begins in a similar way. The shaman seeks out the ancient point of reference such as the stepping stool, tree or a mountain from which she could ascend.

In the shamanic realm, she encounters divinities as goddesses, teachers, and progenitors who offer her direction and advice. "From the perspective of a shaman the non-standard reality that is the soul's world is in contrast to the conventional reality of our awareness , and is totally free of our minds.

The shaman who realizes that all things created have spirits, is also aware that it is possible to communicate with these worldly manifestations by traveling to them breaking through the limitations of space and time. The force of the shamanic endeavor is felt in the manner that it's a voyage of the spirit and that the shaman's soul is returned with the power of the universe. This is the most solid pharmaceutical available."

One of the main reasons for shamanism is that it aims to link the soul with common reality. Shamanism is founded in the animistic belief that all living things on earth and in the universe are souls. are conscious, and are connected.

The belief in animism is in the innate nature of creatures, a belief that souls can exist apart from physical bodies, and that the spirit is the source of our lives and well-being. According to animism, whatever appears, on all accounts to be spiritless, is in fact alive and is a spirit since every thing is living and connected with the spirit. The practice of shamanism lets us connect with the soul, or life power to help us live our lives in the best way possible.

In Shamanism, "force" is utilized to refer to "vitality." Michael Hamer says that staying near-home force is vital to achieving success. Carolyn Myss, a medicinal intuitive, also equates the power of force to life and believes that force is vital to taking care of health and wellness.

"Our beliefs and mental models either positively or negatively, all are manifestations of the way we define and use or not utilize power. There are many people who are unable to access something that has the power of their actions-cash or work, develop an infection.

Our relationship with energy is the core of our well-being." It is essential to recognize the factors that give us power. If we are force-filled or filled with vitality or an important constraint that gives us the ability to live, then there's no place for illness to be able to get into our bodies.

Shamanic View of Soul Shamanic View of Soul

Vitality, force, and soul are described as the fundamental vitality power. It is said that the Random House College Dictionary characterizes soul as "the basis of all thoughts, feelings, and action in man. considered to be a distinct substance distinct from the body. the most profound part of us as distinct in comparison to the physical" Sandra Ingerman refers to spirits as being our "basic essence." Carolyn Myss respects "our spirits as well as our vitality and individual energy are all of the identical power."

There is a belief that Yupik: Eskimo put stock on the divine nature of the spirit, and the spirit is regarded as the source of the existence of. The spirit remains close to your body during a certain duration after death before "heading off to an alien area to await the resurrection."

Every person is a person with two souls. The first is the spirit of their bodies, which are the most basic life-guideline or breath that sustains life and has the real capabilities to take care of the necessities of life. The alternative one is called"fantasy" soul, also known as "fantasy soul" or "free soul."

It's just like the individual, and has feelings and may wander in relaxation or shamanic bliss to "different psychic places". "Free soul" or "free soul" is the one that the spiritual shaman transmits to the higher and lower realms to communicate with spirits or to retrieve lost souls.

Shamanic societies believe that "all illnesses begin by a tense connection to the heavens." The cause of illness is diminished vitality, force or the soul. Somebody or something else can take away our vitality. Soul loss occurs when a part of our vital life force, vitality , or influence comes separated from us due to an injury or accident that is physical or emotional.

The disassociation process occurs which means that a portion of the spirit is removed and continues to live in the spirit world when an event is found to be too intense, and is difficult to bear. Disassociation is a component of survival that helps us survive the trauma.

There are a variety of reasons behind soul loss, including mischances or savagery at family home, such as sexual or physical abuse, denial loss of confidence or self-esteem, loss of a family or friend member divorce, sadness or delayed discomfort, fight with others, with the ultimate aim of fitting in, normal failure, disease, or surgery.

There are many examples of the time when we surrender our souls to other people, in codependence. In some instances, our souls may be taken away by people who do not have their power and rely on the ability of someone else to replace the things they lack in themselves.

The shaman travels through the upper and lower universes in order to locate the portion of the spirit that left and then returns to the individual by blowing it through the mid-section as well as the range of the fontanel head!

The signs of soul loss include dissociation, feeling disconnected from oneself or from the earth self-destructive tendencies, substantial dejection, physical illness and wretchedness. They also suffer from post-traumatic anxiety issue, enslavement , and states of trance.

When we confront lost power or soul, there is an opening which leaves us without destructive energy to fill the gap. This is known as an interruption.

The purpose of an extraction is to remove the vitality that causes discomfort. The negative effects of interruptions include a confined discomfort or an illness like heart problems, the lung growth and stomach and knee pain, exhaustion and interminable pain.

The shaman travels to a other worlds to seek out the spirits to repair their wounds the damage, and following their habits, they perform an extraction, exhort or help the soul that has been lost.

Chapter 2: Reclaiming The Soul

The ability to recover your spirit is essential for vitality and well-being and also to comprehend the motivation behind us and our role in the world. When we do this we can free ourselves from the typical aches and complexities of life, and achieve a sense of joy, fulfillment and peace of mind.

When we examine the lost pieces that we have lost, our bodies become rejuvenated by a positive spirit that makes us completely. When we are complete and are aware of our being part of the divine universe can be realized. In this state it is possible to transform ourselves into a different light and then convey our gratitude all over the globe.

Being an entire person is a deeply-rooted process that requires an intimate connection with our complete personal identity and the mental self. We begin by recognizing that our conscious conscience is speaking to only a tiny part of us as a whole and that it is through our inscrutable making itself known, not conscious self that we can pay an increased awareness of our identity.

Awareness arises from the unconscious that gradually increases to seek out expression.

The uninformed contains data that is unique to an individual , yet is similar to everyone else. Once we are comfortable with its content and its nuances, we can build an actual, fully grown identity.

The self-consciousness of the senses the limiting consciousness of which we're a part of it not understanding the entirety of our incredibly intricate general mind. We are the compartments of the growth of cognition.

In order for this to happen it is necessary to set the foundation of a method that lets the inner self that is cognizant and the oblivious observe the other. Self-awareness is restricted in its ability to observe and requires to become aware of the most prominent elements, potentialities, strengths and attitudes that are a part of the mind of the blind.

The ability to access the inner universe is enhanced through rituals, dreams and rituals, spiritual encounters as well as myths and reflection. In the event that we do not pay attention to this information we invite pathology into our lives via body signals such as gloom, impulses, and stress. Jung highlighted the necessity to blend unconscious substance alongside the conscious mind to enhance the uniqueness of each person.

Dream investigation fabricates cognizance. Deciphering the meaning of our dreams or body manifestations can draw attention to the most important aspects. We learn from the conflicts and challenges we face and discover different aspects to our character. We connect with our spiritual self.

Dreams communicate with the various aspects of ourselves, and exchanging phrases with dream characters provides us a deeper understanding of our identity. Shamanism is a broader point of viewpoint to Jungian notions. Learning is gained by traveling to the higher and lower realms where we debate with top examples, force creatures, and soul guides.

If we do not take information out of our minds or become disconnected from ourselves in any way, we're vulnerable to physical side effects depression, despair and soul misfortune. When we express our life through service and customs We are able to appreciate the world beyond and gain a greater perception of who we truly are.

The universe is an ocean of energyIt was through old beliefs about these planets we first began to ask for help from the midst of chaos and understand the who we were and where we were on Earth. We tried to grasp our own perceptions. The sky provided a regularity of events, like the day and night, and the phases of the moon.

The events were not surprising and were common. The cadenced display of stars in the sky triggered the desires and the constancy of time and desire. The seemingly chaotic events could be considered as a variety of events and photos in relation to a common basis.

Nature was viewed as the cyclic interplay of energy in a common belief system that allowed for the possibility of living a life that incorporated a range of both external and inner events. The process of looking at crystals led me with a larger world of living energy and taught me to see people in a broader and spiritual way.

Soothsaying and Shamanism are connected by cosmological patterns that are similar. Everything within the universe are viewed as living and interconnected. The shamanic tree of the world connects the lower, middle and higher universes of living creatures, earth life and guides for souls.

This is in line with the celestial perspective which planets' strengths are linked to inner mental processes as well as external occasions on earth.

There is a lot of pessimism present and many people do not have the ability to adapt, that's why it causes anger and anxiety. We all take an examination of what we can do to do about negative energy. This Tibetan framework is, by all accounts, the most complex way to manage the cynicism problem in a profitable way.

The Tibetan method of treating despair is highly effective, delicious and transformative. Shamans accept the anger and integrate the negativity into their body. They allow the spirits who dwell on the earth, those who dwell in cemeteries, the haunted houses as well as the ghosts that are ravaging to support their body, and take in the negativity that the shaman has just gotten to his body in a particular way.

They visit the cemetery, the spot in which there are a lot of hungry apparitions. They are devoured and dissected by the frenzied ghosts. The phantoms do what they make a jolt out of having the chance to do, which is consume, but they cannot inspire enough to consume food.

They take the negative energy from the body of the shaman and consume it, and this is considered to be a good display since they're assisting the entire population. The apparitions are then rewarded on a massive scale. This is a fantastic environment model for changing.

The concept of losing your soul across the globe, in a variety of ways it is the same. Trauma, dark enchantment unlucky ways of living dependency, and not living in peace may contribute to different degrees that soul losses.

System

Supporter and I hung out for an hour on her carpet while she put together her instruments. She lit a candle "to discover the path home" and tied the red thread on my wrist. It was her way of helping me find my soul aspects that are not common. She pulled out her sage and cedar mirror sticks to enhance the space.

She applied cedar-wood oil to my shoulders and hair. She then shook her hands around us, and then asked and then shook her head to four heads. I chose a precious quartz stone to be used for the ceremony and then I laid down upon the ground.

Michelle was wearing her hair in a Siberian eye drape that was a headband made of beaded with the size of 118 x 4 cm long pieces of calfskin attached to the headband from ear to ear , and halfway put her face in place. It allowed her to move through the non-normal world. She sat with me and gently tapped her drum for a few minutes.

She started shaking and began to sang her tune. She then reached out to my left shoulder, felt the rhythm in my wrist and then began to stand up in a raucous manner. I could tell that she had entered the shamanic state of consciousness.

She began talking to someone called a spiriting, who helped her release the tension from my body. She measured her hand against my sun-oriented plexus and began drawing out the energy. I concentrated on picturing the energy disappearing from my body.

Shamanic societies are influenced by the belief that illness results from apprehension, disharmony and soul-related unluckiness. Disharmony can be caused by feeling disconnected in some way, such as having lost a connection to the things that have meaning and purpose in our lives.

"Dread causes loss of trust, love and satisfaction that are the primary foundations of health." Soul misfortune occurs in the event of "damage to the unrestored heart, which is the core of one's soul," leading to an array of scattered events.

"In Shamanism, we can see that all illnesses, energetic physical, mental and spiritual, are treated in the same way. No matter what form it takes, the disease is a sign of sickness and causes an imbalance in the life of a man." Shamanism encompasses all aspects of the way it deals with recovering.

The criteria used to select members were as follows: following: They are determined to focus on their worldly healing and growth.

They must be clear and self-aware. They must be familiar with Shamanism and understand how to live in a world that is not conventional. They must be honest when communicating their journeys.

Soul Body Healing isn't about becoming deeply religious or spiritual in an accepted customary sense. It is possible for a person to use Spirit-Body Therapy and also have beliefs about religion or lack of faith in God. It can help you expand the spiritual dimensions of your existence because due to the creative person inside of you is your guru. It can take years of thought and reflection for an individual to come to this point.

Body Healing is about the soul. Body Healing is the fastest path to excellence. In Spirit-Body Healing , we show any person who is familiar with the methods to get to this point within a matter of minutes. In what way would you be able to receive these tiny slivers of light of your soul and these rays of light and apply them to the recovery of your life?

Chapter 3: Guided Imagery

Guided imagery lets you feel the healing of your body and spirit. Through a guided imagery practice using your imagination or imagination are able to enter the forest and butterflies swarm, see the light, and let the face to come to you. The guided symbolism, which is like all the other symbols in this book comes from the tale. These are the steps that people made. For all practices of guided symbolism, ensure that you are in agreement with yourself.

You may take a seat or relax. Take off your tight clothes or uncross your legs arms. Relax your eyes. Give your breathing time to slow down. Take a few deep breaths. Give your stomach an opportunity to expand while you inhale and drop as you take your breathe fully out.

In and out, you'll become more casual. There may be a feeling of humming, shivering or even unwinding. If you do, allow the feelings increase. You might feel greatness, or softness. You may feel your boundaries being pushed aside and your edges becoming more supple.

Now, relax. Give your feet a chance to relax, let your legs relax. Let the feelings of unwinding the muscles a chance to radiate upwards towards your pelvis and thighs. Let your pelvis have the chance to expand and unwind. Let your midriff unwind and let your stomach expand and don't keep it in for any longer.

Now, let your middle-section relax let your heart rate and breathing take place without anyone else's input. Allow your arms to relax, and your hands loosen. Let your neck unwind or your head, and then your face. Allow your eyes to unwind, to see the skyline and dark for a few minutes and let the feelings of unwinding flow throughout your body. Give your relaxation a chance to develop.

If you'd like to check your breathing and let your unwinding unfold each breath. In your own being's image, you are in the middle of a forest and let your energy of creativity, check out the world around you. It's the dawn the most gentle light. The sun is set to rise. The temperature is pleasant and there is a soft morning breeze throughout.

The trees, the earth as well as the atmosphere. In front of you is a path that is soft and free of underbrush. It's easy to feel the woodland floor beneath your feet when you start walking. It is possible to feel the tall grass along the sides of your legs. While you walk within your own being look around! You can see the sun rising. As it rises , you can see the long light beams heading towards you through the dark woodland.

Watch the light emission emanating from the trees. See the air movement in the light pillars and the dampness rising up through the woodland floors and into the stunning white light pillars. Allow the shaft of light and the beauty of the forest lead you to a different place. The bars look as if they come from heaven and are similar to the illumination that comes from God.

In your mind, you observe a large number of butterflies swarming. Watch the swarm move toward you, and then stop at the area at which the sunbeams appeared within a narrow range. Take a look at the perfect circle the light pillars create on the ground of the woods and see the leaves illuminated and their edges shining in the sun's morning light. Consider how the circles of light look like

radiant light. The butterfly is now stopped moving and it forms the shape of faces.

Give your eyes the chance to move slightly and let the world expand before you realize it is expansive and delicate, yet deep and empty. You can feel yourself getting more deep and feel that you are being in a higher further-reaching location. Have a look at the person who shows in front of you. Are you aware of the person behind it? Are you able to identify the Supreme, the preferred mother, your beloved one, a great-grandparent?

Imagine how the face shining; you can see how light is reflected that surrounds the face. It's an amazing view, take the experience and get deeper into the image. See how time seems to stop Feel how the face seemed to always be there. Consider how you've always appeared and also.

When you look of the figure, you'll be able to see it talking to you; the voice can be heard. Pay attention to the words the face in the image informs you of. Then you can notice the figure lifting its arms as if it's praising you. In your own inner self, you feel a gentle light leaving its hands, and then come towards you.

Let the light source come to your heart. On the chance you're required to speak to the figure you have seen. Make a duplicate or contact it via the light source Let the figure know exactly what it is you want and let it know what you're looking to achieve in your life. Feel the love of your heart pour out to the whole universe.

Now, show your gratitude to the person who came to you. Thank them for coming to. Know that you're the most amazing person throughout history who has ever witnessed a stunning vision. Experience your own unique magnificence. You can stay there for as long as your desires. This is a place of healing as well as a place to rest your soul, a sacred space. Take the time to return to your bedroom.

Take your hands and feet off the floor, look up and out the world around you. Your body feels as if it's shivering, brimming with energy. You've looked into your soul and it has healed your body on a level that is deeper and complete. Your beauty and strength are now evident to everyone who has met you. You are able to go out into the world with a sense of joy and enthusiasm and assist all the people whom you meet. Your soul has been shining.

By utilizing your inner self to be able to see the light of healing!

In this session, we will perform an enlightened imagery that will help you let your body relax and allow your soul to recover. Start by taking your breath in deeply and let your stomach rise when you breathe in and then fall when you exhale out. Start by putting your head, let your muscles relax. Give your eyes the opportunity to unwind, your jaw loosen, your neck loosen, and allow your muscles to stretch to release every single one of the tension.

Give your arms the chance to be supported and feel your fingers fall as you let your arms relax and your mid-section loosen. Let your heart rate and breathing consider taking care of your arms. Feel the seat support your body. Feel comfortable by your body, and feel your stomach relax. In your creative energy , you will see an inflator grow in your midsection when you breathe in, and then shrink as you exhale. Now, feel your pelvis loosen Let it go.

Feel it expand and grow. You will feel your body becoming more relaxed as you go into and out. Feel your legs unwind, your feet unwind. You're in a state of casualty. If you are feeling shaking or humming, weight or gentleness, let them grow and unfold more deeply.

Then, in your own inner self, move to a point in the center in your physique. It could be in your stomach and your heart, or even your spine. The middle of your body is a glowing light. It shines bright fragile, like a delicate fire.

In your imagination, you can see the light shining brighter and more brilliantly. The light's light circle will increase in size. Feel the light expand through your fingers, and let it enlarge towards your toes. Feel this soft, warm and luminous light engulf you and hold your body. Now, in your imagination you can feel the light radiating around you, observe the glowing light forming and feel your entire body shining.

Watch the light cross the skin's limits as it grows around you from a step to two. See the light gently whirling and moving. It's a stunner. with a back and forth move and is delicate. it's an emotion that is as strong as your heart. Imagine the moment when this light can transform into the energy of love.

Your body is covered in the shimmer of life and you are being cleaned, mended and adored. The source of this love is a throb that emanates from within your body. Now imagine you are the source of light. This love and this energy are yours. In your own consciousness', increase this light until it is about four feet in the air around you. Now, it's interconnected and converged with the light emanating from the people within you. You are connected and your love melds with those who surround you.

The light will light up when it comes into contact with you. It is then able amplified in its power and flows out from your body. It's exquisite, soft, and beautiful. Your love is transforming around your body and that of the other. It is obvious that you are with someone. is straightforward and you're at peace and elegance. Relax and enjoy yourself.

Relax and allow the light to soothe. Feel the light flashing in your heart. Within you you are grounded in your body. You can feel your body held by your seat. Watch the light flashing within you.

It is the source of your soul as well as your admiration. Once you're ready to go back, look around the room. You can see the entire group that is seated beside you. You are energized, peaceful and at peace; you're deeply regenerated by your own soul.

It is at this point that you begin to heal!

The sight of your soul's vision will transform your life. What is the reflection of your soul within you? Every day life is as simple as a morning. Look up to observe your unique soul that has been enlightened. Whatever way you can visualize your inner vision will reveal your soul's essence to you.

An account, sketch or a joke, a nursery for your patio and an adoration ballad music, a movement or a structure all let you know that there are moments throughout every day that you are sanctified. The moment you look into your soul is when your heart expands. When you see your soul, crying and panting and you feel like you know who you truly are. This is when you begin to heal.

Then comes the final winding, a winding that is full of immense power that combines unity with interconnectedness, iridescence with the Supreme Being and the Holy Messengers! This is about receiving affection by seeing one's entire history as being loved. It's about visionary work and global repair.

It's about changing people' lives to ensure they're incredibly supportive of their community. They are more than capable and also their own. They heal themselves, other people and the world. They're brimming with energy as well as a serious sense of aliveness. even a bit smug about how craft helped them , and how they have to take on new initiatives to help others repair their souls.

Soul Body Healing is a mind-body movement that alters the blood flow, hormonal balance and neurotransmitter levels of every cell of the body. When the soul is glowing it impacts the psyche through changes in demeanor and the body through invulnerable body improvement. The study of how the soul heals is usually focused on the ways that feelings, thoughts and images alter the blood flow and the hormone balance within the body.

The examination as a principal body medicine has significantly improved our understanding of how man's mental state and his world view affects recuperation. The examination has contributed to the integration of various systems such as reflection as well as unwinding, guided symbolicism and integrating into the standard restorative treatment when it comes to ailments, such as malignancy or AIDS.

The experience of a lifetime is perceived as a signification for those who feel Spirit-Body Healing. They see events as pictures. The woman who witnessed the essence in God within the butterfly crowd, saw the picture. The images can be all five faculties, or each one without any delay. The person perceives the event as a thought as a feeling or thought or even a sensation of a sound or vision or both.

The moment does not have to be clear or resemble an action film in power. It could be similar to an innovative idea. It could be visual, audio-related, tactile, olfactory or gustatory. Images of the most amazing encounters are initially analyzed by the brain regions that control thinking and organizing the development of muscles.

The release of neurons comes from the memories of the vision as well as the actual process that makes the image more authentic such as the creation of the work. The way it is felt to the viewer can be described as if an image, idea, or a visual of a supernatural experience comes from somewhere else or their mental psyche. For certain people, it feels like it comes from their creativity or memory.

Many believe that it is a result of the Godhead or the soul. Because profound experiences are outdated and involve many open motor and tactile pathways they seem real and real as one is able to reach them. Our bodies have evolved to be repaired by otherworldly fantasies.

We believe that some of these memories of images or events are not current and were gleaming within the human mind when it advanced. When these dreams reach the heights of our awareness and then disappear they are a remarkably recovering background. There have been dreams of spirit and Gods from the most recent recorded history.

Healings have been associated with these visions.

The dream changes the physiology of the brain to bring about the recovery state. When the person is able to connect images within the brain for the task of making a piece of work or constructing a patio garden the muscles develop that result in a high degree of fixation.

The process takes an individual's whole attention and frees them from the worries and stress from the outside world. It happens naturally. The individual doesn't have to do anything except to focus completely. The neural pathways that were previously in the psyche are able to take control, and the person is transported "somewhere otherwhere" into a state of complete concentration, which the majority people experience after meditation.

The three ways in which spiritual experiences affect each cell of your body!

The spiritual images cause the termination of the neurons in different areas in the brain. The brain's neurons that have been terminated of movement that are falling connect with what remains within the body, in three primary ways.

Spirit changes your sensory system

Images stored in the correct mind trigger the hypothalamus. The hypothalamus stimulates the autonomic sensory system , which result in a state of the sensation of relaxation or excitement. two-fold adjusting framework that affects the whole body and touches to the point of touching every cell.

The autonomic sensor system is a healing structure that regulates and holds in check the blood stream and pulse rate breathing rate, the level of hormones required for any move we're doing.

It's also the framework which we need to repair. The framework was believed to operate without input however it is recognized as not being substantially affected by thoughts within the mind. The autonomic sensor system has two parts: reflective and parasympathetic.

The intelligent part of the autonomic sensor system is the one that regulates "battle and flight" so the physiology is crucial to stay away from the tiger, or be able to accept the cautious posture.

The view of the wide areas of the equator mind of the person who is at risk warns the hypothalamus. It triggers an intense excitement, and also accelerating the heart rate, increasing breathing, delivering blood to the vast muscles that inundate our bodies with hormones of anxiety and adrenaline creating a physiological system of preparedness.

The experience of fleeing from the danger, escaping from a tiger or battling it and fighting back and eventually getting away is the entire experience. When you're out of danger finally, the sense of safety eases stress and puts you in a position of relaxation. The process has been referred to as the discharge/excitement cycle. It outlines each individual's strategy for responding to any situation which is stimulating.

However, the activation by the parasympathetic portion of the autonomic sensor results in the unwinding of, recovering repairs to the body and preventive assistance. The cerebrum's image of a calm scene of a deep vision of creating work and ingenuity, or praying, alerts the hypothalamus and triggers an adrenaline rush. The pulse slows down, circulatory strain decreases. Breathing becomes less strenuous and blood flows to the digestive tracts, and the whole body is transformed.

The movement or vision of a gentle touch strengthens the circuits that recall the profound unwinding process that makes up this the physiology. The physiology now consists of repair, of creativity as well as of petition.

Spirit changes your hormonal framework

This model provides us with an understanding of how our brain functions with the body , and the way that muscle movements and images can affect our entire being. When an individual is in significant event, the part of the cerebrum which holds images of the development of muscles is animated and transmits messages to the hypothalamus, which allow us to be able to react to symbols.

If the scene is one of deep satisfaction or a onset of strain, our body is put in a state of healing through the hypothalamic pathways of our parasympathetic sensor.

When the patient experiences torment and the vision is observed in a way that is interesting, the pressure around the pain is felt, and then released. The unwinding process follows and the healing processes of physiological framework is initiated. The spiritual experience influences the body's hormonal structure.

When nerve cells release, like an intricate machine of light, which glistens in the cerebrum, our hypothalamus transmits signals towards the organs of adrenal in order to release adrenaline, epinephrine, and various hormones. They circulate throughout the body. They are then absorbed through receptors that cause certain cells contracting, some to relax, some for demonstrate, while others are left to rest.

The whole physiology of us is altered a second time due to an experience in the soul that is a vision or an event stored within our brain. The second alteration is a result of caused by hormonal changes. This is less pronounced, but it is just as significant as it is every cell of the body.

If a person is able to see the Supreme or the Blessed Mother, it alters the hormone stream for every cell in her body. The changes in her circulation and beat, her respiratory rate, as well as the flow of blood to the cerebrum and the heart.

Spirit alters your Immune structure

The third way that experiences of soul impact the body, which is located within the realm of the neuron-transmitter. In this case, the experience of the spirit world affects certain regions of the cerebrum to release endorphins and neurotransmitters. These affect mind cells as well as the cells of the immune system. Neurotransmitters ease stress and help the secure framework function more efficiently. They trigger T cells that are executors to consume cancer cells and white platelets to fight infections and , in general, alter the body's ability respond to illness.

When a person is having an obsession with his soul, and creates music or art and moves, or creates a scene that is euphoric and liberating The body actually alters its physiology to repair itself. The onset of endorphins after experiencing the dream of our soul is an extremely enjoyable experience.

It's like a man working out. Endorphins can be described as sedatives, or medications that alter the brain and make men feel a sense of being encircled and at the same time loose, bouncing and shivering. They also make him feel calm. The capacity of endorphins is similar to chemical compounds that alter the personality to enhance and enhance the sensation, making it even more real.

In reality, the release of endorphins during dreaming and supplication could be the true healing power. Psycho-immunology is a word that connects psychotherapy for the brain and neuron for the nerve nets in the brain, as well as is invulnerable to the framework that resists to show the ways that thoughts or images in the brain impact the framework that is safe. It is also known as Spirit neuron-immunology because soul influences the secure framework to function at its best and consume cancerous cells, infections, and various trespassers.

Soul Body Healing utilizes the core concepts that of support, onset of anxiety or a change in state of mind and feeling connected. Sole Body Healing as well as Care groups are similar characteristics. The soul's dreams that people can see are ones of mind-set, of adoring and respecting oneself. The profound experiences of people have provided an immense amount of support.

Knowing that you are loved by Jesus is the greatest motivation for a man who is a Christian. Spiritual dreams also give the importance and logic to the man. Carl Jung said that his patients who believed in the Supreme and also believed in a resurrected existence following death had better lives and cured their ailments over those who were skeptical and had no faith in the afterlife.

He stated that irrespective whether God was real and existed and that a huge beyond or resurrections were shown this belief was helpful to those who needed to recuperate.

The soul's healing power is released when the life force that is derived from the total awareness. The soul enlightens us with an inventive process which is youthful and vibrant. Repairing, power energy, vitality, and cognizance are all the same.

Within the Hindu religion Vitality and matter are recognized through awareness. Vitality and matter are inside awareness. When one recovers from the soul, they travel to the point of awareness , and then slip past the outer layer to the place that is the heart. If you experience recuperation feelings of vitality, you are energized.

There is a release of vitality that can be perceived as a humming shaking, or a vibrating. It is an energy that flows throughout the body, from the body to the body, and from all over the world to our bodies. It is viewed by psychics and devotees and is frequently depicted in the form of visionary work.

The vitality is known as Chi, prana, Kundalini, God's breath and needle therapy meridians for vitality and chakras, as well as the life-limiting factor It has been depicted throughout the years and has been an essential element of human existence.

At the point that you are able to see the light of your soul vitality is also included. Perhaps the most straightforward illustration of Spiritual Body Healing would be that it releases our body's vitality that is mending to flow. The soul departs to home, returns, and reconnects with the deep source and vitality is released as a flowing waterfall. The brightening of the soul releases vitality.

Find a light within the darkness!

Find the primary light to be visible in your unconscious. Examine your life for spiritual messages or positive thoughts to appear to you. We understand that this can be difficult and appears impossible to imagine when you are suffering from the deepest pain. But, as it happens that when Gina was able to taste her food and said it was delicious and delicious, she also got the first glimpse of the heart behind the dish.

She saw the part of herself which could see the beauty of her and who was beautiful. Find the light that surrounds you in your deepest darkness. A large portion of people who shared their tales of recovery to us also looked to their own resources.

We have heard from them about using books, reflections, and other skills they gained through their lives before they came to be ill. The knowledge you've accumulated can be useful to you today. Everything you've done throughout your life has provided you with an ability that is crucial in your current repair.

If you've learned about computers or cooking classes and attended ladies' gatherings, moon-bundles or even taken classes on reflection using your normal job, take advantage of the main point of all that change now to give yourself the chance to change and grow. Sway to dreams, the shamanic and creative work, or something similar. This journey in Spirit-Body Therapy will be a journey through your inner world, into the dream world.

Both shamanism and creative work are the best ways to take your fantasies and making them real for you. In shamanism we are referring to traditional methods of seeing the your soul, which include intuition and imagination, as well as wandering into a fantasy world as well as seeing inner, symbolism endeavors, and making repairs to work.

Shamanism isn't anything new or strange; it's the traditional method of experiencing soul that has been able to attain for hundreds of years. If you can bring the fear of torment and confusion to the outside, so that you can think of it as the result of a dream or vision the process begins to speed over your healer.

If you compose it or draw it, then move it around, it grows and shifts from fear and confusion to a new voice and a clearer vision. In the process of taking an interest in things, pain can be the chance to shed your previous self. It's the process of shedding the Chrysalis. In the unconscious, a small light is reflected.

Begin to embrace this light and hold still for the dream that can change your life. Explore your options and find the right person to help you get to the next level. Find craftsmen, companions as well as healers and teachers. They are derived from the most traditional people throughout your lifetime.

They may come from unplanned places. Do not judge them! Learn from the lessons and experiences of those the people around you. The learner's mind is a great thing. The feeling of shock is wonderful. Accept that it's a process that will require some effort. Keep going, allow it to take place. This is only the first step towards recovering.

Utilizing your imagination to the most of your entranceway, and then get it back!

Find a comfortable place. You can sit down or relax. Untie tight clothing; cross your arms and legs. Shut your eyes. Allow your breathing to ease. You should take a few deep breaths. Give your body a chance to rise up as you take into and lower while you let your complete breath out. When you breathe in and out, you'll appear to become more casual.

It is possible to feel feelings of humming, shivering or winding down. If you feel this way, let your emotions grow! There is a possibility that you feel a touch of weight or a gentleness You may notice your limits becoming less rigid and your edges becoming more rounded. Now, let yourself loosen.

Give your feet the opportunity to relax by letting your legs loosen. Let the feelings of unwinding to expand across your thighs and the pelvis. Allow your pelvis to unwind and open. Now, let your mid-region loosen and let your stomach expand without holding it in anymore.

Now, let your mid-section rest and allow your heartbeat and breathing to take place. Give your arms the chance to relax, and your hands loosen. Let your neck unwind or your head, or your face. Let your eyes have a chance to unwind. You will be able to observe a skyline and the obscurity of a second.

Relaxation is a state of mind that you can give the chance to radiate throughout your body. Give your relaxation a chance to develop. If you would like to count your breaths, and let the unwinding continue with each breath.

From this secure place of unwinding in your imagination, travel into a state of suffering physical. It's a place of pain that holds an intense tension, fire, or irritation swelling. It is possible to visit that spot and begin there. In addition, you can examine your body and find a weight, void or a thin layer, an opacity and a physical feeling of a sense of dread.

Furthermore, visit the place where the pain is and breathe to that spot gently slow and slowly. Inhale, and let your being, you take a trip to the spot and relax there, allowing any images or thoughts to arise. The trick is to allow yourself to be and allowing them to unfold. Give the image an opportunity to be a manifestation of a painful experience within your own life.

If you suffer from illness It could be something that happened in the past, before you realized you might being sick or could be something from your past. It shouldn't be the most painful experience that you've had, but it could be something that caused you to worry. From the safety zone that you are currently in, reverse your steps to the moment. Think about it as clearly as you are able to.

Be aware of how your body feels as you walked in the surrounding area, note any scents that are present and hear the noises around you. Remember that you aren't here now, you're in this room now and what you allow to happen is the memory. Allow the memory to take over you. Feel what it was like to be in that pain. Let the agony go, and release it outward.

Remember that suffering is a pathway to get more grounded. While you are experiencing the pain and confusion, let your inner strength grow. Feel it develop inside you. Feel the vitality of your body grow and aid you through the time of suffering. When you notice the way your body feels when you hear sounds or view images, keep an eye to any other memories that arise.

If you have more mature images or dreams, or more established memories that pop up to you right now If you think that they're not too difficult to recall, do it today. As you breathe in them, feel there for a second take note of the way your body feels as you breathe, feel the air, feel the breeze, see images and hear voices. Allow yourself to completely be present. Be aware that you aren't there physically.

You are safe in the room, sheltered by your prayers. If you would like to, imagine someone you love and trust flies along with you in the dark and remains with you as a guarantee and in your midst.

They'll see nothing happening that you cannot handle. If the darkness makes you feel uncomfortable, return to the room and block the room , and then get your eyes open. Just do the things you can handle.

It is possible to try it at a later time. Now, look around you for light sensation, a euphoric feel or a sense of closeness. Take a look with a clear eye direct into your own experience and determine if you see a flash of light.

Look around Behind you, and unanswerable! Find a watchman an angelic messenger, or a proximity. Spend your time in the dark looking for the first glimpse of light and support.

In the event that there is a sound, here's telling you that you've been given the voice the chance to speak! If you do not see or feel an enthralling glow and back, remember a time where you felt light and awe-inspiring happiness. It could be during a moment of prayer and reflection. Or it could have been something you observed during a walk in nature, or a feeling that you felt while creating work or playing with your imagination.

Find that feeling or moment of joy and light and fully engage in it right now. Similar to what you experienced when you were in the midst of darkness and darkness, you can immediately enter the experience of happiness. What is your body's sensation with joy and lightness? what do you notice and smell or hear, and feel?

Recollect the atmosphere; your own experience in which you the feeling was that of being in the presence of the utmost brilliance. Now, for a moment, go back to the place of darkness! Give those feelings a chance to resurface and, now, with anticipation take a step forward until you are greeted with awe and joy.

Let go of the darkness's thoughts Let them receding into the darkness, disappear, and be tested in the light. Then, perform a reverse and forward several times. Now, stay in the beautiful sunshine and allow it to take over and repair your. Consider all of the emotions of joy to let them flow over your body, cleanse you revitalize you, and get your wounds repaired.

Be aware that you have the ability to go from the darkness to the brighter side. Know that it's safe and beneficial to enter your haze and remain there. You are able to safely enter the haze, and the thoughts surrounding it and gaze at the surroundings and feel those feelings while letting them fade away.

Utilizing your own inner awareness to help you become bigger than the pain!

Find a comfortable place. You may take a seat or lie down. Take off your tight clothes; uncross your arms and legs. Shut your eyes. Give your breathing time to slow down. Take a few breaths. Give your stomach an opportunity to expand when you inhale and lower as you breathe out. When you inhale and out, you'll appear to be more casual.

It is possible to feel feelings of humming, shivering or unraveling. If you do, allow these feelings grow. There is a possibility that you feel the awe or delicacy of it and you might feel your boundaries easing and your edges becoming more rounded. Allow yourself to relax. Give your feet the chance to unwind, and let your legs loosen.

Relaxation is a state of mind that you can give an opportunity to radiate over your pelvis and thighs. Let your pelvis have the chance to relax and open. Let your stomach unwind and extend your tummy. Allow your mid-section to relax. Allow your heart rate and breathing take place without interference from anyone else. Give your arms the chance to relax, and let your hands to relax. Give your neck the chance to relax, let your head unwind, and your face unwind.

Give your eyes the chance to relax; look at the skyline and dark for a moment. Let these feelings of unwinding an opportunity to take over your body. Allow your unwinding expand. If you want to, take a moment to check your breathing and allow your unwinding progress with each breath. Concentrate on what is that is the most significant thing in your life that has a lasting impact on you.

It could be physical ache, intense anxiety, tension, anxious feeling, gloomy or an illness or infection. Pay attention to it, allow it to be present wherever it is in your body, feel it, then breathe in it. Allow the desire or feeling to manifest, and let it grow. Rekindle it as a fire watching how the remains of burn.

Allow the insurmountable to be present, allow despair to be present wherever it is. Do not let yourself be down and allow the feeling of suffering to take you completely. Allow it to dwell within yourself, feel your personal suffering. Be aware of it, experience it, and study the cause of your suffering.

Take it on, get towards it, move into. It is pulsing and has a reason to serve, it's alive. Do not ask what the reason is, but take a moment to be in it. Let it reveal itself to you in its fullness. Let yourself cry and shake, shout, or be a twitching, and allow the torment to release itself into your body.

Find the place in which the agony has the greatest strength and thickness and where it expands with force, like dams that are about to slam. It's amazing; it's like experiencing the tempest, experiencing the power of lightning and wind.

Imagine the scene in your head glowing, the inner scene flashing and shattering. You can go into the place that is shattering, and let it shatter into millions of pieces. The area before is being exploded.

Give your body the chance to shake and shake. Let your agony be a part of you and acknowledge it, respect it, and be grateful for it. It's your teacher. It will lead you to the stage of your life that will change you to the time of death.

The feeling of suffering is what will make you want to recover. The desire to ease the suffering will force you to go on a new path and live a life that is completely different from the way you've lived in the past. The main thing you should do is be there.

Go to where it is in the flame, and don't let it go. Look towards it, stop fighting with it, do not avoid it, let it to be. Breathe into it and embrace it. Be able to look at it despite your pain. Find out who's face it is. It's an accurate assumption that she is ten years old age, or twelve years old. age. Is it an image of someone you've lost?

Draw it, it's shocking and disconcerting and it could be the essence of a spirit that is evil or the source of disgust, the source of the sharpness. Now, look into the darkness surrounding the pain. Feel the gap around the pain. Feel the emptyness and feel the empty feeling of being isolated from all others.

You are in the place where the torment is. It's like staring in the darkness of the night. You're brilliant, but you are lost in the obscurity. It's like being on the spaceship of a rocket You are unweighty, indistinct, and your awareness is wide and vast, and the pain is in it.

From the torment, completely from the blue you're huge and you are in a three-dimensional space in which the pain is. You are in a location that is passing , and you're about to be created. This is the moment before birth. Mull over the pain. Let it have its own life of its own Give testimony about it, and cease fighting it.

When you allow torment to move about the inside of you, you will see an open space in the rock. From this obscurity the void serves as the catalyst for making art. It is not overwhelming by the agony anymore. If you reach the point of no-light and you allow the pain to wander around. It's completely in the universe and all. This is the moment where you experience the absence.

The inability to let the suffering be on its own is difficult and you're a part of it, and it's difficult to let it go. You can see your suffering turning into a burden within the vast space. You will see it become smaller and see it making an impact on your life.

Making use of your inner-self's ability to dig deep into your being to bring it towards light!

In your head, you can imagine an event that you felt strong and secure. The event could have been a triumph or moment of love or even the first meeting to your child, an extraordinary perception. It is important to find one event. Explore the area thoroughly; be between the events. Slowly slow down, use all your faculties. See it and feel it, touch it, smell it.

Get assurance, helpers and companions and then go to a location that's dark and sombre.

This could be due to your health or an illness from the past fear, or the death of someone you love.

Furthermore you can, with insurance, visit the same place and then go back to the date and look at that time the full length of your choice. Now imagine that there is a gap between the place of brilliant illumination and the one of darkness.

Journey through that passageway from the dim area to the bright spot. Take the dim place and head towards the meaning of peace and perfection. It is possible to do this until you find yourself in your personal darkness.

It is not necessary to worry You can remain there and examine what's boring for you. You can at any time you'd like, leave and return to your peace.

Chapter 4: Role Of The Shaman

The social position of a shaman can be described as a set of interrelated rights, obligations, and behaviours as conceptualized by people in a particular social setting and as a expected behaviour of the context of a person's status and social standing. There are today many misconceptions in relation to shamans' roles and responsibilities.

The Roles

Shamans play different functions in society. Shamans could play as healers in different shamanic communities. They acquire their knowledge and ability to heal through the realm of spirits. They enter Spirit World to gain knowledge about it. The majority times they have several assistants or helper entities from the realm of spirits. They're usually spirits that take the form of animals or the spirits of healing plants. Sometimes, these entities are also the ones who left the shamans, or their other ancestors.

As a method of healing they enter inside the bodies of the person who is sick to combat the spirit that is responsible for causing the patient to become sick. They treat their patients by eliminating that infectious spirit.

Additionally, there are numerous shamans that know about the plant that is native to their area. They also make use of herbal remedies to treat those who are sick.

Mediator

Shamans are also mediators within their cultures. Shamans are thought of as people who connect with spirits.

for their communities for their community, and this includes communication with spirits of deceased people. In different traditions, their roles as mediators can be demonstrated through their objects and symbols. Shamans act as mediators between religious entities as well as ordinary people. In certain cultures communities, they are also known as soothsayers or seers, mediums, astrologers, palm readers, and many more diviners. They play various roles in the society. In some societies, they have the ability to do amazing feats of magic.

Other Roles for the Shaman

In Siberia's Reindeer Tungus Shamans are the people who possess the power to control supernatural entities like spirits. They also can stop spirits from causing damage to the people around them and at times they can act as mediators for spirits.

The Tungus Shamans, who could be female or male, use specific tools, such as tambourines mirrors, costumes and various tools.

They travel into the realm of spirits, they perform rituals for their own clients, and groups in general. They can also locate lost objects, identify the reason for a person's health issue, give a specific ability in certain conflicts, and even predict the future of events.

Shamans' primary function is to ensure and restore harmony in their communities. They conduct rituals of protections as well as blessings, divination, and hunter magic. They also treat illnesses due to spiritual roots, like spiritual contamination; spiritual intrusions; curses and souls lost. Shamans are also known as the guardians of the ancient cultures. Because of their understanding of the ancient traditions, across many times, their advice was sought after by a variety of.

Chapter 5: Shamanism Beliefs

Shamans communicate with deities and spirits not only through prayer , but as well through rituals and offerings and through direct interactions with spirits.

They are also found throughout time all over the world. They fulfill roles that are crucial to the community or society to which they are a part. There are also fundamental beliefs in shamanism that all shamans across the globe share. These fundamental beliefs are crucial because they bring the comfort, wisdom, and meaning to millions of people from different parts of the globe.

A very popular beliefs in shamanism is that everybody and everything follows the same pattern, and therefore they are all connected. Everything around us is connected to one another. Shamans believe that the existence of an alternate reality is real. It is usually called"the time of dreams" in the spiritual realm by traditional people or as a non-ordinary reality for contemporary mystics..

The Beliefs

Shamans also believe that certain people are able to attain the state of consciousness, and also to access the other world to heal of oneself and other people and for solving problems. This belief is usually supported by a fervent and very strong desire to personally experience an alternative reality.

A major aspect of eloquent beliefs in shamanism is the existence of spirit guides and helpers that live in an alternate reality. Although modern mystics tend to not adhere to religious institutions, they believe in Jesus from Nazareth as a powerful spirit teacher.

The majority of shamans also proclaim their faith in different kinds of godlike supernatural beings and consciousness. Additionally, for they believe that everything inanimate and animate , is infused with soul or a particular supernatural spirit.

Another shamanistic belief pertains to being a part of something called a Vital Force, or an unpersonal power that is present in many things and manifests as a vital force in some living beings like the chi of Chinese and Polynesians, the mana and prana of yoga. the Baraka belief of Muslims and the number of Kalahari bushmen.

Also, they believe in the existence of a a personal energy body exists , and is perceived by other people by way of an aura. It can also be enhanced by the energy centers within it, referred to as meridians and chakras within the Eastern concept.

Shamanism actually is based on the premise that the world we live in is infiltrated by invisible forces or spirits that have profound effects on human lives. Shamanism is also a subject that requires particular skills and knowledge that is individualized, and is a different form of religion from those known religious beliefs.

Chapter 6: What Shamanism Believes Have To Do With Spirit And Soul Concepts

According to the shaman, every child, woman and man is connected to their family members as well as to other human beings and to all forms of life and all elements of nature , which includes animals trees, clouds wind trees, rocks minerals and even the entire earth.

The principle and practice of shamanism is that it is in a position to improve the health of the planet and personal spiritual development, and to promote connections and increase the power of.

Shamans think that the universe is composed of two major realities : the ordinary and the common. The former is referred to as the physical universe that is connected by space and time and the other is the spirit world that is not visible to the naked eye.

The Concepts

Shamans they are the missing link in the

the realm of spirits. As we face environmental challenges in the present, we need spiritualists now more than ever before. The future of the world as well as the future of the earth depend on their beliefs and the wisdom and faith.

Shamans are taught through their experiences as well as through the guidance given by others. One of the most obvious differences in the case of other mystics, healers and Shamans Shaman is the path they take, which is often described as"the "flight through the spirit". In an altered states,

Shamans have the ability to travel into the world of non-ordinary to seek guidance and wisdom from the wise spirits to assist in healing and aiding the everyday world.

The primary goal of each Shaman is to maintain and restore harmony and balance in order to stop suffering and suffering in the world. When shamans step into the world of the other they perform soul retrieval. They enter the state of a trace and leave the body to search for the traces that make up the essence of the individual. If you've had the chance to go through numerous losses of soul during this life time, the shamans can aid you in recovering your soul.

Shamans believe in spirits and they play an important role in human society as well within an individual. They can communicate with the realm of spirits and carry out rituals of healing. In the world of spirits, they are in a position to retrieve one's soul.

Your soul is in fact your soul's essence, and it's the way your immortal soul's molecules link to your conscious and physical bodies. But, that connection may never be restored and so is its essence. This essence is conscious and can decide to go away due to certain situations. The concept is generally known as soul loss.

If this happens there is a chance for shamans to help you recover your soul. According to the shamanic perspective the majority of illnesses lead to loss of soul. It also happens when there's a breakdown in the connection between the spirit and you and also the break between the nature and the human.

To retrieve your soul's spirit, the shamans go on journeys to locate those parts missing from your souls. You must be able to negotiate return and help you reintegrate those pieces that are separated.

Understanding Entheogens

In other words that shamans are traversing the axis of mundi, and are entering the spiritual world by causing transitions in consciousness and entering an state of ecstasy, which could be induced by autohypnosis or by the use of entheogens.

If you're trying to figure out what is an entheogen it is a psychoactive compound that can be utilized in shamanic, religious or even in a spiritual realm.

Entheogens can also be used to enhance a range of different methods that are essential to revealing and transcendence. These include psychonautics and psychedelics as well as meditation and psychedelic therapy. magical art and visionary.

What is it?

Entheogens have been used in various rituals over long periods of time and their spiritual importance is firmly established in the latest evidence and anthropological research. There are many examples of Entheogens, including cannabis, psilocybin peyote Ipomoea tricolor Amanita mucaria, ayahuasca uncured tobacco, and Salvia divinorum. In the formal or traditional religious structure Entheogens can be considered valuable psychoactive compounds, especially when used to achieve spiritual or religious purposes.

Entheogens are among the most potent psychoactive substances that are utilized by the shamans. They have also been utilized throughout the ages for different reasons, including ritual, medicinal or spiritual, as well as recreational and more. It is a crucial type of psychoactive substance which is utilized not just by shamans but as well by other people because of its capacity to trigger a specific type of experience in the consciousness of an individual. This is one of the most effective tools utilized by shamans on their journey into the realm of dreams.

The utilization of an entheogen is widely used in healing practices, and this is due to the influence of spiritualists. The psychoactive compounds have been utilized as a vital instrument for promoting the various kinds of understanding and learning. Entheogens can also be utilized to trigger transcendent experiences and, in the present the word "entheogen" is the most commonly used term for the intoxicants shamanic.

Entheogens are essential plant ingredients and when they are consumed they give individuals with a mystical experience. There was a time when these have been described as hallucinogens and psychotomimetics. These substances are extremely important as they can cause, or aid in identifying with the feelings of others or experience an experience of feeling connection to other people. Due to the nature of these substances, they are used effectively in shamanic practices of entering the spirit realm and healing people or restoring their souls.

Related Music and Songs

There are numerous songs and songs that relate to the practice of shamanism. Music and songs of the shamanic tradition contain both music and songs that are being used in their rituals and rituals. The shamanic rituals are actually rituals, not music that creates a the musical aspect.

When it comes to the shamanic religion, shamans are also able to play more active roles in the musical world opposed to mediums involved in spirit possession. Shamans have various ways of creating sounds. The sounds they create serve a distinct purposes. Drumming by shamans as well as their songs in particular are important.

Although many shamans utilize drumming and singing and other instruments, it's important to keep in mind that shamanic practice isn't a formal musical performance, but rather the music is directed towards spirits, not an act of offering their listeners.

The Music

The rituals they perform are a sequences of actions, and their focus is always on their perception that of spirits. They also use music and songs to connect with spirits. From a musical perspective the rituals that shamans perform have distinct discontinuities.

There could be interruptions that occur due to different reasons. Sometimes, this is because of the difficulty of communication with the spirit of the Shaman that requires him to call other spirit. The rhythmic aspect of their music in their rituals has been linked to the notion of incorporating nature's rhythm and then magically re-articulating them.

The music and songs that are associated with shamanism typically consist of instrumental and drumming which are excellent to meditate. These can also serve as extremely relaxing music for many. In addition the music and the songs of shamans can be very soothing for the mind and soul.

There are many Shamans who mimic animals and birds. They have a striking ability to incarnate and continually changing their outer and inside appearance. In their ritual time they talk and singing musically. They speak to their spirit guide, and conversing with them.

- 21

They are also able to mimic the voices of birds and animals and also their spirit guides.

The most distinctive characteristic of the activities of shamans is an intimate connection to music and art. Shamans are singers and guardians. They transmit the technique of singing from generation to another. As they listened to the ceremonies of shamans, people also learned how to sing as well as their sound row and also their melodies.

If you take a listen to music and shamanic songs you'll realize that they also function as a reflection of their talents and needs, their preferences, habits and thoughts. When performing shamanic rituals it is possible to discern the meaning in their lyrical power as well as the lyrical pages of the music they play, nuances of their song's lyrics and the gorgeous harmony of their music.

Chapter 7: The Tools Used In Shamanism

To perform these rituals, they require a variety of different instruments used.

shamanism. These tools have proven essential for shamans, not just when they perform their rituals, but also during their journey to the realm of spirits, or when they perform rituals to retrieve souls or heal souls.

Tools

The Drums are the power of rhythm. The rhythmic force of drums can be similar to the heartbeat of the earth and is embedded in shamanic rituals.

Shamans travel on the beating of the drum into the realm of spirits, and then return with force. Drums, in conjunction with a rattle, is an essential part of their craft.

Rattles are brimming with power and function as an antenna for power. In many areas of the globe the use of rattles is alongside drums, and in the region of Siberia the rattles are usually included in the drumstick or. They are extremely simple to carry around and may appear to be simple tools , but they extremely effective. Rattles serve a variety of purposes in shamanism. They can be used in various rituals to help consecrate holy places and can also be used to the gods as well as to help heal.

Mirror of the shaman - this tool is utilized by many spiritual practitioners to travel and energetic protection healing, divination and healing. It's a round disc, and is used by many shamans to tool in their healing treatments as well as other tools that are essential to the practice of shamanism, such as drums and rattles.

Incense is a tool that can communicate with one's soul and senses. The smoke that emanates from this device can be used to invoke blessings and cleanse ritually. In addition to the rattling, the drumming and singing smoke is a way to build an effective ritual. In some shamanic practices that use smoke, they also use

- 24

Different kinds of incense are an important part of their culture.

Flutes can also be used in a variety of rituals involving shamanism. They are easy to use.

Flutes are also great to aid a shaman's shift in their consciousness. This type of instrument isn't just utilized during rituals but it can also be utilized when shamans go to the realm of the spirit.

The Staffs are tools that play an important part within the practise of shamanism within different cultures, and most significantly in the

Scandinavian magical tradition. It is also used to record a precious carved document of a long and difficult journey. It is a symbol of authority, and acts as a support, as well as a weapon.

Orgons is an exceptional place in which shamans are able to communicate with spirits. It is a crucial place to communicate both with physical reality and spirit.

Orgons are among the most important tools used by shamans, particularly for use in Siberia as well as Mongolia for every tribe that uses these tools. Orgons are available in a variety of designs; they can be carved from wood, decorated with leather, or mounted on wooden hoops . They can also be constructed from metal materials. They are also the home of spirits, and shamans can pass them on over generations as spirits live in these.

Shamanism is a central theme in Folk Tales

There are a myriad of stories, myths, and folk tales from all regions of the world. Every country and region has its own story to tell that reflect their culture and way of life they lead.

These literary works are passed through generations and have helped the readers today comprehend the world of their forebears and the people who lived before them throughout the entire world.

Shamanism is widely practiced throughout the globe and there are many forms of folklores that mimic the idea of Shamanism. Shamans are generally viewed as a person who is spiritually chosen who is in touch with the realm of the supernatural and the magical which is why it could be concluded that witches may fall under the category of shamans. It is crucial to remember that experiencing death is an additional phase in the initiation practices of the shamanism.

Folk Tales

In a variety of folktales that are well-known like "Hanses and Gretel" there are rituals of initiation that are among the major hidden themes in the story. Although this story is usually considered to be a symbol of the rite of passage but there are several underlying elements that resemble the universal shamanic initiation idea.

Additionally, there are different shamanic themes throughout Georgian folktales, as well as on the pages of American Folk tales. Many stories from these areas focus on spirituality as well as the spirit world and the ability of a person to transcend the world to the realm of spirits. They're performing rituals and incantations to heal the people as well as the characters in each story.

Folk tales, like other types of literature, share universal truths that are their hallmarks. The central themes that are revolving around the concept of shamanism that are found in many folk tales across the globe are a sign that, even in the times of our ancestors or those who wrote these tales from the folklore the idea of shamanism existed. Shamanism's idea is a universal concept and has been around for a long time.

Variations Per Region

Shamanism is recognized as a collection of ancient beliefs and practices connected to spirits. There are many kinds and variations of shamans from all over the globe and they serve diverse roles and different rituals.

There are three distinct types of shamans , namely the White, the Yellow and Black. They are the Black Shamans and the White have a long tradition, and the Yellow Shamans are the results of the influences of Buddhism.

It is crucial to remember that "White" as well as the "Black" designations do not necessarily signify good or evil. They simply mean that they working with different types of spirits. In the Siberian

Tradition dictates that every direction has an assigned color, as well as the colour of a shaman's skin is determined by the direction in which they is able to gain his strength.

Variations

Black Shamans are known as the most powerful of shamans of their group and gain their strength and strength by observing that of the Northern direction. They are regarded as warrior shamans, and are able to defeat evil by fighting against might. Black Shamans are examples of discipline and bravery.

Based on historical precedent the shamans have the ability to fulfill their duties the midst of battle or war, as well as in moments of peace. In times of war, they increase the morale of their troops and also perform rituals that aid during each battle. The power of the army was linked to them, and they were always recruited the midst of wars.

If there's peace they are able to serve as excellent advisors

conducting foreign policy by making alliances and advocating peace. In time of the Mongolian Empire, the entire agreements were ratified at ceremony of shaman.

White Shamans get energy from Western Direction and, due to this, they channel their prayers to their Western Heavens. White Shamans are able to build strong relationships with the nature spirits and are also known as spirit of peace. They focus on calming the spirits that are angry and concentrate on helping humans maintain harmony with nature. They also offer divination and blessings, but there's one thing they aren't able to do and that's the curse of the shaman.

Within the Mongol Empire In the Mongol Empire, Shamans were involved in local affairs , and also served the administrators , they are equally concerned with the daily life of

The people.

Yellow Shamans - Between the 17th and the 19th centuries between the seventeenth and nineteenth centuries, Tibetan Buddhism or the Lamaism had been imposing itself on

Mongolian people, and at this time, it became difficult for the Shamans. The Black Shamans would not accept foreign

The White Shamans and their religions were separated. There were those who

They resigned their lives to Buddhist authority and were made the Yellow Shamans.

The White Shamans, along with the other White Shamans, refused to cede their beliefs.

Shamanism is still practised across a variety of nations. In fact, it's an important practice among Huns, Altaic people, Uralic as well as Udmurtia as well as Mari-El. It is also being practiced in Korea especially within South Korea where their role is typically performed by women known as mudangs. the male shamans are known as Baksoo Mudangs. There are various shamans in each country and region , and they play a important part in the society they are part of.

Chapter 8: Relationship To The Pachamama

Awareness Platform

If you discover that there's some mental system that doesn't permit you to see the realm of the cosmovision due to the fact that you're ensconced to a mental framework that is restrictive. This structure is limiting and blocks any attempt to learn about the wisdom of Shamanism that is rooted in the past. In order to progress you'll have to broaden your Awareness Platform

But what Is an Awareness Platform? The term "Awareness" refers to the fact that an awareness Platform is a specific lens, a method of seeing reality which a vast majority of people rely on and is marketed in the form of "unique fact".

"Science" is an example is an Awareness Platform.

Shamanism can also be a Awareness Platform.

If you are interested in entering this brand new Awareness Platform and wish to know more about the significance of what we've stated, you need to do Ritual Na 3. We expect that the new Platform will enable you to experience a greater version of yourself. It which will let you gain access to a greater version of yourself and will allow you to be capable of changing the perspective of the most difficult and difficult events in your life.

Ritual No 3 - Awareness Platform.

Na 3 Ritual Na 3 consists of writing down on paper reasons that lead you to explore Shamanism. The reasons are why you're not able to accept this holy spirituality. For instance, you could say: "I'm afraid to change to a different way of thinking, as if I change my perspective on things, then my peers are going to judge me" Or "I'm terrified to be involved in Shamanism since I would like to stop my studies and if I do change my mental outlook and interpreting the world, I will not be able to meet the social obligations I have". You could also write, for instance, "The members of my family will be afraid and will cease to trust me".

Write a new document that reads: "Nature will guide my steps".

Then you can you can light an candle. Only burn the margins of the line that reads

"Nature will direct my path". Write down the date. Thank Nature for greeting you.

Burn the Fear.

After performing this ritual you'll have created the date of your start in the Noble Way to live your life. You will also have conquered your fears for good, forever.

Then you can embark in a journey of opening and development.

Learning

In our modern Western society, we're not familiar with the ways in which we relate the difficult circumstances that happen to us to the immense learning that comes from life. We're not at a point where we are thankful for the difficult circumstances that come our way. Also, we aren't trained to be aware of the infinite wisdom that these situations produce for us.

In the Shamanic communities The idea is to learn from each loss in order to build on the previous defeats, since -according to this perspective, the sufferings are there to learn from.

We don't know what a blessing it is to us to be in these painful experiences.

Instead of focusing on the "complaining" anxiety, depression, paralysis and insensitivity, the communities encourage us to look for what is the Great Learning of each loss and every disappointment.

In the next phase, we will perform an exercise to comprehend the significance of what's been spoken.

Ritual No. 4

This is a ritual that helps us think about a difficult time in our lives. In order to do this, we have to select the exact event. For instance, the death of someone dear to you or the onset of a disease or injury or move, etc.

The third goal is to keep the scene in its context and try to recreate the scene. The key questions to consider are: What age was you when the incident occurred? What was the location? What actors were who appeared in the scene?

Recall how you first reacted to the incident. What was your first reaction? What was your initial reaction? How did you feel? What were the questions you asked yourself in that moment? What type of thoughts came first?. Think back to the times when there were feelings of guilt, desire or nostalgia, or supplications for a return to the previous state.

The next step is to reflect on the moment that followed, maybe just a few days or so after it. The most important questions to ask yourself are what have you needed to alter in the past? What decisions and thoughts did you think about in the years?

The fourth and last task is to reflect - from the present - on this important process of personal growth caused by this painful experience. The main questions to consider are: Do you believe that this experience has triggered a change in your character? Write about the most significant learning(s).

Put the paper in an unlit candle and then leave it in the candlestick. It's a wonderful reminder to never overlook the important lessons of life. An experience you will not forget.

Thanks for the Education

The Shamanic masters inspire us to gain knowledge from each difficulty, however, they also encourage us to be grateful for what has happened.

The speed of everyday life and the constant absence of time in cities make it challenging to cultivate gratitude.

We must remember to give thanks, and to do this, we should establish a new habit. An habit that is integrated into our lives daily.

The importance of gratitude is paramount in Shamanism. Every thanks serves as an opportunity to remind ourselves that things could have turned out differently in the way they have. Giving thanks is, in the sense of paying respect to Mother Nature for the path that took place.

In this view that thanking is a ritual. A ceremony that is designed to preserve the harmony of the Natural balance, beginning with an insignificant symbolic gesture. Within this fragile balance, every action needs to be mutually beneficial. Should the Gods of Nature allowed such something to happen it is important to thank for their help.

To gain a better understanding of what we've just stated, we complete this ritual.

Ritual No. 5 - Thanks Ritual

The following ritual is simple, yet very profound in the same moment. The idea is that beginning today, you develop the habit of saying thank you prior to and after taking part in every step of your daily life. The times will be: half a block before and half a block after whatever you do.

If, for instance, I am happy with the job I do and am just half a block away from starting my job, I need to stretch my hands, relax and then say: "Thank you for this day". When I get back at a about half-way to my point of departure, I repeat "Thank to you today".

Another example is if I love dancing and would like to learn to dance be a better dancer, I'm grateful before enrolling in the dance class, and grateful when I leave.

Decide to give thanks at the beginning and throughout the times You will discover that by doing this you'll never lose your humility or passion, two allies you should never lose. .

Requesting to Learn

If we are thanked and when it is asked for it is imperative to perform it in a reciprocal manner. This kind of exchange avoids over-use and therefore helps to prevent imbalances.

Reciprocity creates correspondence and understanding and deters insensitivity.

In the Awareness Platform of Shamanism, when it asks for the Earth to be a part of it, it's not asked "simply" however there is a dialogue. Something is left up to nature. Forces of Nature. This is a thing that is logical to you, and that Nature can absorb. For instance, you can plant an edible fruit over the earth.

We believe that the relationships that we have with Nature will be a sure thing of being extremely beneficial for humans: "if you place a handful of seeds on Earth and you get an entire tree".

Here's a test to help you understand it better.

Ritual No. 6: Exchange Ritual

The Ritual Na 6 encourages us to create interactions with Nature. The primary idea is to be able to contribute to Nature's Natural

Forces and that you will see the benefits. To do this, you need to utilize a container that is in your possession or you can create it using a container or even a big bottle. The basic concept is that the pot has soil, and within it, you are able to sprinkle, for instance the seeds of the fruit you typically eat (Mandarin and grapefruits, as well as avocados, loquats and more.). It is recommended to water the pot or at a minimum, place the new container in a location that is prone to rain. After a couple of months, some will sprout. You will find out the amount you made by planting the seeds you put in the trash can.

In the symbolization of process of learning

We've recognized the value of learning from the painful moments , and we can also see the importance of saying thank you to for them.

Now we'll see the importance of identifying learning with a title.

When we name the entire course and allowing us to use the word anytime we require it without having to go through the long and tiring process of the time to learn.

For a long time, we have written on a piece of paper which was a lesson learned in an extremely painful moment of our lives. However, the learning is extremely long. For instance, I might declare: "From going through this disease, I realized that I needed to be able to accept myself, comprehend my past and where I was born and I must not delay myself ever again for the sake of attracting interest".

The idea is to link this learning by using a single phrase or two. For instance, in this instance, it is in my mind the words that I could relate this knowledge include: "Approve yourself" or like, "I approve myself".

To become cleat in order to be cleat, we must set an example to allow us to grasp the reason behind it. A woman, going through an extremely significant experience -nothing more nor less than an improvement in sight- realized that for her, nothing can be more satisfying than the pleasure which led her to keep taking pleasure in the vibrant blooms and hummingbirds which fly magicallyclose to them.

She linked this learning to"Color. "Color". In naming that word today she is able to recall everything she learned from the process without going through the same emotions over and over repeatedly.

To better understand what it means To better comprehend the meaning of the word, we will follow these rituals.

Ritual No 7

The ritual is designed to help us create associations between the large learning and smaller names. It is thought to make it an extension to Ritual 4.

Do not forget this Ritual No 4 consisted of writing the important learning on paper and placing them in the candle holder to not lose it.

The next step is to use the written document with the amazing learning and put it in a the word that has meaning.

This meaningful word will increase your confidence and will allow you to use it anytime you require it.

Time Duration

The timing to be Shamanism.

The past is presented to us as a thing that is that is a given, inaccessible, formed, inert, unchanging. We are told that our past was the place we came from and we've been told that it's a point without return.

The wisdom of Shamanism encourages us to work within the frameworks of Time.

Shamanism transforms the idea that we have a "past" and leads us back in a way that is mystical, and to heal.

From the viewpoint of Shamanism In the Shamanic perspective, we have to learn from all circumstances of our lives. However, there are times that are so painful that they do not let us be able to. It's crucial and important to seek to heal these wounds.

Shamanism permits us to draw time lines, to go into a very difficult time of our lives. It is best done with care and discretion.

This isn't a form of play or a game, and should not be treated lightly. It's a process that begins as an imagined practice, or used as a visual representation can have very pronounced consequences.

It is only to be used only in circumstances that warrant its use, situations where the individual really has to go back in time and restore it.

We emphasize that we don't have to make a complete change to our past, nor alter an entire year of our lives or even a month, perhaps not even a single day. What is required is to change that dangerous circumstance or event that has caused deep hurt.

For healing, I need to go back in time.

I'll have to recreate the scene over again. However, this time I won't be required to explain or analyse it on my own It will be required to visit the scene in order to be able to transcend the moment.

It's like reliving the same scene over and over again, and then changing every scene that I can remember. This will make a new past.

I have to open the doors of these painful moments so that light can be able to enter. I must also let the air out using the finest scents I keep on hand each piece of my memories.

So, the long-simmering darkness will be gone and light will return. Every scene will be charged with new colors and shades. There will be gaps filled in and spaces will begin opening to new, lasting learning.

It's then about returning to the past in order to make past. A past that is aligned and beautiful and enables the building of a peaceful future.

Rituals

Ritual No. 1 - Recognize the existence of all Beings.

Go to a spot in which a natural setting prevails. It could include a park, shores of the ocean or a river, an area of forest that is not in cities; an natural setting close to a road or an ecological reserve. It could also be the national park.

When you're there take note of all the birds there.

Select one to examine in greater detail (if it does not appear during the ceremony, you are able to select another).

As an observer, you can be an observer, and try to be as inactive as you can. Try to identify it. Make an effort to explain its appearance and color. Be aware of the things it does. If it eats, it is looking for things to build its nest when it's in a group. Try to discern his song and try to take in the scenery.

If you are capable of accounting for your experiences, strive to be as close as you can and with the greatest degree of sensitivity and compassion.

At the end of the session, you should write on an article "My appearance is not impartial". Write down something important you experienced when the greatest rapprochement with your chosen species was achieved.

Ritual No . 2 Recall that God is God in all beings.

Go to the place where nature dominates. The plan is to take an "walk of appreciation". This is the act of walking around all the time to take in the beauty of Nature. The idea is to take in the scenery completely, freeing us from anxieties, and revealing our own perception and identifying aspects we have not considered of Nature as well as of ourselves. It is worth it to stand in front of an insect web, near the butterfly's flower as you contemplate the blooms that the flowers produce, observe the insects that live near their habitat, to be awed by the shapes of stones, and everything else to be done with contemplating the beauty of Nature.

If you take this walk more than 45 minutes , and be attentive to the various issues that we've raised, certainly you will not be able to delay knowing why we say that God is everywhere in moving beings.

If you could identify it, after the walk, thank God for to the Earth. By doing this you'll be able to thank God and the Natural Forces for just passing through.

Ritual No 3 - Awareness Platform.

Ritual Na 3 consists of recording the reasons you've been exposed to Shamanism. This is the reason that you're unable to accept this spirituality that is sacred. For instance, you could record: "I'm afraid to change in the fear that if I alter my perspective on life, I'm afraid my family and friends are going to judge me" or "I'm scared to engage in Shamanism since I'm trying to finish my studies and if I alter my mental outlook and interpreting the world, I'll be unable to fulfill the social obligations I have". You could also write, for instance, "The members of my family will be worried and will cease to trust me".

Then, you should write a second document that reads: "Nature will guide my steps".

Then you can ignite the candle. Only burn the margins the sentence that reads "Nature will direct my path". And then write down the date. Thank Nature for greeting you.

Then , burn the Fear.

By performing this ritual you'll have arranged the date of your start for the Noble Way and eliminated your anxieties.

Then you can begin in a journey of opening and development.

Ritual No. 4

This is a ritual that helps us think about a difficult time in our lives. To accomplish this, we have to select an event that is specific to us. Examples include the death of an individual close to us or the onset of a disease or injury or a relocation, etc.

The third job is to recall the context of the event and try to recreate the scene. The key questions to consider are: What age was you at the time it occurred? Where was it that it happened? What actors were who appeared in the scene?

Recall how you first reacted to the incident. That is, what was your first reaction? How did you react? What was your reaction? What were the questions you asked yourself during that time? What thoughts did you have first? . Do you remember if there were feelings of guilt, desire and nostalgia, prayers to return to the former state.

The next step is to reflect on the moment that followed, possibly 3 or 4 days following it. The key questions to consider are: What have changed in the past? And what thoughts and decisions did you think about in the past few days?

The fourth and final step is to reflect - from the present - on this vital process of personal growth caused by this painful experience. The most important questions to ask yourself are: Do your consider the experience brought you some knowledge? Write down the most important learning(s).

Place the paper on an unlit candle and then leave it in the candlestick. It's a fantastic reminder to never overlook the important lessons of life. An experience you will not forget.

Ritual No. 5 - Thanks Ritual

The following ritual is easy, but profound in the same moment. The idea is that beginning today, you develop the habit of saying thank you prior to and after taking part in each day's activities. life. The times will be: half a street prior to and half a block after the activity you select.

If, for instance, I am grateful for the job I do prior to starting my job, I should stretch my hands, relax and then say: "Thank you for this day". On my way back to the office, when I'm only half-way from my location, I repeat "Thank to you today".

Another example, if love dancing and would like to learn to dance be a better dancer, I'm grateful before taking the dance class, and grateful when I leave.

Decide to give thanks at the beginning and throughout the years and you'll see that in this manner you'll never lose your humility or enthusiasm; two friends that you should never lose. .

Ritual No. 6 - Exchange Ritual

The Ritual Na 6 encourages us to create interactions with Nature. The primary idea is that you can be a part of the interaction by utilizing nature's Natural Forces and that you are able to see the advantages. To do this, you need to utilize a container that is in your possession or you can create it using a container or a large bottle. The idea is that the container is filled with soil, and within it, you are able to put, for instance seeds of fruit you typically consume (Mandarin grapefruit, grapefruit, avocados, loquats, grapes and more.). Make sure to water it or, at the very minimum, put the pot in an area that receives rain. After a few months, some will sprout. Then you can see how much you've made by planting the seeds you put in the trash can.

Ritual No 7

This ritual compels us to create associations between the large learning and small names. It is thought the possibility that this could become an extension to Ritual 4.

Keep in mind the fact that Ritual No 4 consisted of writing the most important lesson on paper, then placing them in the candle holder to not lose it.

The next step is to use the written piece of paper that has the most valuable knowledge and connect it to an appropriate word.

This meaningful word will increase your confidence and allow you to use it when you need it.

Chapter 9: Shamanic Skills

The most effective method get started as a spiritual shaman to train under one. People born into shamanic families usually taught into shamans. They are taught by their family members or teachers from their group.

If you aren't part of a group like tribes or families or clan, you must find your personal instructor. It's a blessing that shamanism has gained popularity again in recent times. Therefore, you can look up shamanism-related workshops on the internet. You can choose to take an online course or enroll in a live class.

You can do it by yourself however, it's not easy to learn through trial and failure. A guide with experience will help your progress quicker as they will teach you the correct way to perform things and avoid making mistakes. Learning by yourself is less expensive and you can do it at your own speed, but.

Be aware that just going through a book or taking part in one of the workshops will not make your into a true shaman. It takes a lot of time to master shamanic practices and much more to be considered an actual shaman. Many train for their entire life in a constant process of learning and continuing to learn.

Shamanism isn't a pastime or a means to earn fame or wealth. It is a commitment to make relationships with the spirit and to be a part of the community. People who wish to become Shamans are frequently tested by the initiation process and other events within their lives. Only those who can pass these tests will be granted the power they desire This power should not be used to achieve selfish goals but for the benefit of.

The Training Process

Shamanic classes are usually held in isolated natural locations. The students are removed from the common responsibilities like their work, families and leisure, technology and other such things. This is so that they can concentrate fully on their training.

Apprentices might be required to observe a strict regimen and eat only the prescribed foods and drinks. They may also be required to follow certain rituals, such as meditation, rituals, or exercises over a long period of time. Some of the rituals involve communicating with spirits, or going through trials to demonstrate the worthiness of one's efforts.

The study of plants can require going to places where they are discovered and then experimenting with the plants. Some teachers allow their students to take a bite of the plant in order that they will be acquainted with the plant.

Finding the Right Shaman

There was a time that the rumors of shamans spread by word-of-mouth. The stories of their ancestors, often turning into legends. In the present day and age there are many shamans who are offering their services to more people. You can find their advertisements and blogs on the internet.

While it's easy to find Shamans these days, it might be a bit more difficult to locate someone you can believe in. At one time, shamans were popular because of the work they performed, but the advent of technology and media generally has made it much easier for people to appear to be people they aren't.

Before selecting a shaman to assist you, verify their background. Does this person have a history of involvement in any scandal or crime? Do you have feedback from the shaman's former clients? What are they famous for? What is their character? What is his/her way of dealing with people?

Keep in mind the following:

Learn more about the methods used by the shaman and specifics. What is it that he/she does? Are the tasks performed in a setting with a group of people or on a one-on-1 basis?

There are shamans who specialize in particular areas like healing ailments, breaking addictions dealing with phobias, restoring energy balance, reclaiming the soul's fragments and more.

* The shaman that you select is based on your preference. Certain shamans impart knowledge but others don't. You should

inquire if they're willing to teach you, and what they need to be taught.

Take into consideration the qualities of a shaman. They must be genuine and reliable. Do not trust anyone simply because they tell you to, even if the person claims to be powerful.

The real shamans might possess the ability to do something however they don't let it swell their self-esteem. They realize that pride can hinder their ability of being able to perceive reality and communicating with the spirit realm effectively. They do not push others' boundaries, but they keep their respect. They accept people even with their faults.

* They won't pressure hiring them, they allow you to visit them at any time you'd like. They radiate a calm aura.

* They must be open. Find out how they became a Shaman. They should be able of telling you a true tale of how they changed into one. If they reacted defensively or you saw inconsistencies their statements it could be that you are speaking to a fraud.

In the end, you should listen to your gut. If you find something concerning the shaman that bothers you, do not pursue the shaman any more. There might be other teachers or Shamans who could be more suitable for you.

Visualization

Shamanic activities require lots of visualisations, and you need to become accustomed to visualizing things in your head. It's great if you dream in pictures or do a lot of daydreaming If not then you should engage your imagination more.

* Visualization Exercise 1.

Find a storybook with illustrations and take time to look at the illustrations. Remember your childhood experiences as a child , when your parents read to you fairy stories. It is possible that you will remember more than just being able to hear the words, but also the images and the emotions that occupied your brain. Remember these moments while you read your fiction.

* Visualization Exercise 2.

Take a pencil and paper, then sketch the letters I and Y in front of each the other. Watch the Y some time, before covering it with one hand. Look at the letter I, and imagine it breaking in the middle to form letters Y. Visualize one of your arms getting taller than the other. The same thing can be done to the opposite arm.

* Visualization Exercise 3

It is a good idea to take a break from your eyes and imagine everyday objectslike your smartphone, your watch, your car and the list goes on. Visualize them in the greatest detail is possible. You could look at them first before you can see them in your head or create the images solely by recollecting them.

• Visualization Exercise 4.

When you're in a place that is crowded and you will see a lot of people, observe them as they conduct their job. If you see someone passing through, pay attention to them and hold their image in your mind. Think about where they might be and what they might be doing in the future. Take note of what else you think of.

- Visualization Exercise 5.

Select a painting, drawing or photograph you are drawn to. It's best if the photo isn't a hassle and easy to understand. Find a peaceful spot in which you can sit for a while without distraction. Relax in a comfortable spot and breathe deeply to let your mind unwind. Look at the picture for a while, focusing on your thoughts. Make an effort to recall every detail.

If you are ready take a deep breath and recollect the image. Write it down in your mind. Make sure you can see the pictures as words and images. Take a look at the image. What did you recall correctly? What was missing? Close your eyes and imagine yourself merging into the image. Explore the surroundings, take the stroll in your new surroundings and interact with the creatures and things you meet.

The Power of Psychic Awakening

Certain individuals are born with strong psychic faculties, however, they are not nurtured by everyone. They can, however, become developed with the practice. If you'd like to become a shaman, it is essential to develop your psychic abilities in order to see the realms in which spirits reside.

In order to develop your psychic abilities first, you need to utilize more of your senses first. It's because the information you receive from psychic sources can be converted into a sensory experience such as a visual, a feeling, sound - within your brain. If you are a habitual oblivious to the five senses that detect, it's likely that you'll overlook the sixth sense's perceptions up.

Make a point to pay more attention to what's happening in the surrounding area. Pay attention to the surroundings. What do you see all around you? Are things as they would expect them to or do you notice any oddities? Are you seeing something you aren't used to seeing because you're occupied with something other? Choose an object that is interesting to you. Do you know what it is made from according to its appearance? What does it feel when you touched it? Will it make a sound when you hit it? What flavor could it have when it's been made edible?

What do you hear? It is possible that you have shut out the noise of fan or traffic because you've become accustomed to these sounds. Check them out again. Can you tell if they are making soft or loud sounding noises? Can you discern some melody? Are there any sounds that you can hear but can't discern the source? What is the possible cause of these sounds? If you hear voices of humans Can you tell if the adult or a child is making these sounds? Are they female or male? What's their character like?

Feel the gentle breeze blowing over your skin. What's the temperature like? What is your temperature when compared to your body's warmth? What do you feel in your clothes? Take a walk around the floor using your feet. Without lookingaround, can you determine if you're standing on a flooring made of hardwood, cement or soil, or even sand? You've probably looked at flooring before, and are aware of the type of floor but are you able to come at the exact same conclusions even if you don't look?

Make it seem like you're once again a child. Everything is brand new to you, so everything seems exciting. You don't know what it is, means and why there are no judgments about them. When you are able to fully observe and not blocking your attention with worries or internal dialog you'll get more information from your senses normal as well as your psychic senses.

Utilize all of your senses, and expand your senses to the world beyond your senses. The above exercises initially focused on things that you actually feel However, it later focused on imagining things that aren't available to you right now. Test this out with different objects and then see if you got it accurately. The more you try this and more often, you'll be able find clues that you're getting real psychic information or constructing your own based on preconceptions. It's a long process time and trial but once you get knack of it, it'll be worthwhile.

In the process of awakening your psychic abilities, it is a process that you perform with your mind. This is because there exist universes that are not accessible to the physical senses, but accessible to the mind. Through your brain, you are able to travel to the past as well as the future, travel to places further away, and even create objects and spaces from nothingness. Mindpower lets you make and discover different worlds.

Your mind is able to make up fantasies that are dismissed as not true. But, your mind can explore unimaginable realities that exist in that they can be recognized and shared with others. We will discuss these types of realms later.

You need to build the ability to develop "shamanic eyes" or a different way of looking at things making use of more of your senses and your imagination. You have to be able to accept that the things you imagine might be true at some degree. You'll grow more shamanlike this way.

Consciousness Levels

It will be much easier to identify and improve your psychic abilities if you know where the psychic information originates in your subconscious mind. Three levels of conscious involved in the development of psychic abilities that are the conscious mind, the subconscious mind and the superconscious mind. They all are able to balance their messages from one the other, ensuring you are healthy and safe.

Your mind's consciousness is the one responsible for reasoning, analysis, and making decisions. In order to be effective it must maintain the objectivity of its mind and eliminates information to focus on what it believes to be crucial.

The subconscious mind functions as a computer , which takes in details that are not in the conscious mind's eyes. It becomes too overwhelming for the conscious brain to process every aspect of your experience, which is why the subconscious mind keeps these things in the same way as books in libraries. But, if your subconscious mind is stimulated by necessity, meditative exercise or psychoactive substances, or relaxation, it may send beneficial information and information back into your conscious.

While your subconscious is powerful by itself, it's an element of a larger, more advanced and more intelligent mind - that of the supraconscious. This is thought of as the one universal brain from which the intuitions, insights psychic signals, and spiritual wisdom are derived from. Though your subconscious mind is a the repository for your personal experiences and concerns but it also functions as a connection between your own consciousness and the collective and everyone else's. Some people consider this to be the collective consciousness or Akashic Records.

You can access your unconscious mind through constructing your imagination and directing your thoughts. You should stop being consumed in your mind's thoughts and snooze your inner dialogues and just listen to the other things you are able to see.

Utilizing Your Psychic Ability

The abilities of psychics can include visions (clairvoyance) as well as sounds (clairaudience) and sensations (clairsentience) as well as smells (clairalience) and taste (clairgustance). It could also manifest in forms of feelings (empathy) or thinking (telepathy). Sometimes, you might have an understanding of something. this could be described as intuition.

The ability to psychically communicate requires clearing your mind as thoroughly as is possible. Everything that is left in your consciousness could affect what you see. If you're scared of something, for instance you might see frightening spirits in the vicinity. Take 5-10 minutes to clear your thoughts.

If you've reached an altered state consciousness, concentrate on something you would like to learn more about or ask your inquiry. In complete silence and wait for the answer. Your subconscious mind's answer could be in the form of memories of visions thoughts, symbols as well as sounds and other.

It is likely that your imagination can make up scenarios based on your thoughts, desires and preferences, as well as biases fears, desires, and worries. That's why it's essential to remain at peace, not judging and detached from the outcome. If you are unable to perceive any thing, don't try to try to force it to happen, instead, you should slide into a state of rest. It is possible that you are experiencing an unfocused look because a portion of your brain is fighting against psychic signals. The more relaxed you become and relax, the more your subconscious mind will lose control over your mind.

Make a note of what is in your thoughts. This can be done through a recording device or by writing notes. Just gather the information you need without analysing them until later.

When the flow of information is slowing or if you find yourself trying to make sense of what you are seeing to be true, stop recording.

It is possible to realize that psychic perceptions could be literal and straightforward however, they could be vague and symbolic. Once you've gathered the psychic data, it is possible to shift back to the reasoning analytical part of the conscious mind. You will now identify the psychic impressions. Do your best to interpret them even if you aren't sure of the significance. In the future, you can gather more details about the person you're trying to locate the answers to your query. Examine whether you did the answer right and also the areas where you may have made mistakes.

In the end, you'll find patterns that assist you in understanding the significance of certain psychic signals. As an example, it might discover the subconscious's "word" for positive news is a vision of a feather, and for bad news is like a rock. Based on these insights, you can build a psychic dictionary that assists you in interpreting psychic signals.

Being a hollow bone

The power of the shaman does not belong to them. The shaman is merely an embodiment of an "hollow bone" which allows the power that are inherent to the soul pass through and manifest into our world. This is why being completely empty is essential to becoming a powerful shaman.

The self is the self that constructs a false world, a false one which makes life more predictable and convenient. It's comprised of the person you believe you are , what you think you are and what you believe about how the world should work. Things that hinder you from getting psychic information , like the fear of being judged, your biases and expectations are the result of your self-image. These beliefs and stories could stop you from doing what the shamans do.

This false reality is strengthened by accepting it as fact and then promoting it to others. When this belief is challenged, we respond with anger and refusing to accept other viewpoints. To see the shamanic truth it is necessary to avoid accepting this false reality and self-deflection.

What you think you're is merely a construct and there is a real self that is experiencing your experiences but isn't a part of them. Be aware of the inner self that is watching the events instead of just being present and then relating yourself to them. Be the unrestricted awareness that can take you to other worlds.

The more you empty yourself and become more real, how authentic the experiences turn out to be. If you fail to be empty and see the world through your eyes, then what you experience will be distorted and filtered through your own preconceived notions, beliefs, biases and other factors. You must step away from them, however it is possible to revisit them following the journey. It takes time to master this process and the more you practice the more comfortable it becomes.

Create Sacred Space

An area of sacred significance is a place that is physically accessible where you can do your shamanic practices. Different traditions have specific guidelines for what the sacred space should appear like. You can choose an established tradition and adhere to the guidelines, or simply choose a location that is inspiring at ease, secure, and comfortable. It is important that it serves the purpose of being a place which connects spiritual and physical dimensions.

The place you choose should be one where that you can do your tasks at peace. It is best if there's no distractions.

The space should be filled with objects which are required for your job or are important to you. Do not clutter your space with unneeded items.

Make use of candles and dim lights. Avoid using bright lights as they could hinder you from entering the trance.

If you're looking for a relaxing experience, you can listen to soothing sounds like natural sounds, soft music.

Acquiring Protection

Shamans invoke spirits of protection to help them travel as well as other tasks. They can ask for their help during rituals, particularly when they are fighting an attack or curing an illness that is caused by an evil spirit.

Shaman armor is a possibility to wear as a form of ritual clothes that have objects with beneficial energies and beneficial spirits.

Mirrors are a great way to deflect attacks and harm targeted at the shaman. In addition you can utilize any item that signifies protection for you.

Staying with a Habit

Shamanism is full of potential, which is why it has been around for quite a while. It is also diverse enough that there are thousands of different practices to pick from. However, you should beware of the temptation to switch from one type of practice to the next without fully mastering all. It is through practicing and engaging deeply in the realms of the unconscious that allows the spiritual shaman to access the power which bring healing and transform.

These are the most important techniques for working with shamanism. The next chapter focuses on journeying shamanic to the realms in which the work can be done.

Chapter 10: Shamanic Journeying

A shamanic voyage is the process of moving from normal reality and into a shamanic one to communicate with spirits, obtain energy or recover it or collect data. It is typically done using drumbeats that are played on the back of your mind. A lot of cultures believe that the sounds of the drums can help the shaman reach an altered state of mind and guide his/her soul to the direction he or she wants to go.

Many even view the drumbeats as strings that connect the listeners and take them to different realms. the Australian aboriginals identified this as the Dreamtime and the Celts consider this to be "the Other World" and some see them to be parallel universes.

In certain rituals, the drums are played with rattles, and other instruments. The shamanic songs known as Icaros are often sung well.

The journey of a shamanic experience involves entering a state of trance in which Theta brainwaves dominate. You can identify this as an euphoria that is between wakefulness and sleep.

Plant medicines can be utilized to produce more powerful effects. Shamans can learn about the plans they should utilize from previous shamans and from the spirit of plants themselves. The belief is that some plants contain strong spiritual beings in them. For instance, they refer to Ayahuasca "mother Ayahuasca". Apart from that, Peyote, Salvia, Magic Mushrooms as well as Iboga, the San Pedro cactus, and Iboga are all possible options.

The 3 Worlds of the Shamanic Journey

For the Shaman There are three worlds that are linked to one another and are identical to one another. These three worlds make up the legend of World Tree that is believed in all religions. In the Lower World forms the roots of the tree, while the Middle World is its trunk as well as it's Upper World is its branches. It is believed to be the central point of the universe. Hence, it is also referred to as the axis mundi , or the world axis.

While the image of a tree might provide an impression that the Upper and the Lower Worlds are not connected however, they actually do. According to the legend, as you go higher into through the Upper World, you will be located in The Lower World, and if you sink more and further in that Lower World, you will be within The Upper World.

It is possible that everyone are able to travel on the axis since it is a part of the soul of each one of us. The universes that it connects are basically conscious levels of consciousness. Even though the events and experiences within these worlds don't happen on an physical level, they're not inaccessible. Humans did not create these worlds. They found them and then looked into these worlds.

It is possible that these realms exist within the collective unconscious of the human race. It is something that as humans all share and is in our minds, regardless of whether we are conscious of it or not.

Every world has its own unique characteristics so the kinds of items that can be obtained from every world can differ from one to the next. The inhabitants and the sights of the world also have distinct characteristics. Each area requires a distinct set of abilities and level of consciousness from the tourist.

It is essential to know the distinctive aspects of each realm to be aware of the place you are. Also, you must know how to navigate between worlds with ease.

The axis mundi is the place where the three worlds meet It is also where the veils which separate our world from the shamanic realms are less making it more easy to travel between the three worlds. The axis is a mythological phenomenon However, there are many representations of it in our world. In the end, the axis mundi links the various worlds so you might see it in the real world too. Find places in nature with an ethereal quality to them. It is important to feel calm in this place.

Visit this location either physically or through your mind. See the surroundings through shamanic eyes, or an eye of your own mind. Make it your goal to access the realms of shamanism through this space.

I. Lower World

This Lower World is often confused with hell, however you won't see monsters, flames or demons here. It isn't an area of suffering This is the place where the rejuvenating nature's energies reside. Here, you can be in touch with the elements of nature - spirits from nature, water and land formations and the elements of fire, water air, earth, plants and animal life, just to mention several things.

Learn from plant and animal spirits within this world. They may bestow positive characteristics on you - like the speed of the Cheetah, and the strength bears for instance. They can also teach you about healing. You might be taught by students or try your hand at interacting with plants that you see in the and you can eat these plants at your discretion and observe the effects.

Because it also addresses "roots" it is possible to consult with your ancestors, and participate in the history of your tribe here. Spirits of the deceased often end up in this place. Shamans searching for lost souls come here to search.

When it comes to the mind the lower World is akin to Subconscious Mind. It is concerned with habits, feelings, instincts and dreams. There are trials and obstacles in this realm, but there are also spirits of help to help you conquer these challenges.

People who have traveled to this world have described it as an earthy natural habitat, like a forest or forest, cave or rivers. If people are present the area, they are likely to be indigenous tribes or cavemen. There is usually no evidence of modern technology in the area. There are numerous animals roaming around freely.

How to Get into the Lower World

The Lower World can be entered by imagining a scene in the natural world.

* Locate an entrance point that leads deep into the earth. It could take the form of a cave a burrow for animals or volcano or a hole in the soil, like manholes through an open log or hollow tree or when you dive into a water pool.

You may be more at ease with the familiar methods of transport You could imagine being on a descender elevator or an escalator. It is also possible to imagine climbing a flight of stairs and sliding along an inclined slope.

II. Middle World

The Middle World is the non-physical dimension of the world that we inhabit. This is where our awake reality takes place and also where we can use our normal consciousness to.

This realm is accessible for the purpose of finding answers to various global issues, including relationships or financial problems. Because this is the energy counterpart to this physical realm, the shamans travel here to search for missing objects and even people. Remotely observing locations and individuals is possible here. Shamans can also try to interact with or influence individuals in this dimension.

If you want to be able to see the nature in its purest nature can visit The Middle World.

Be aware this: Nature here is distinct than the lower World In the lower World, Nature exists in its raw form, as well as the animals are archetypes or the oversouls of the individual creatures. It is the source for nature's energy, therefore it is more powerful. The Middle World, the nature essence comes from physical world, which means it originates from living beings as well as natural structures. When people visit our world they could develop a greater respect and appreciation for their environment as well as improve their comprehension of the natural world.

Shamans looking for cures from the world of physical visit this location to discover what they require. People who hunt wild animals or seeking out special types of plants visit this planet.

It is believed that the Middle World is the most chaotic of all the worlds. This is also where the majority of the spirits who are confused are located. They are the souls of the deceased that do not realize they are dead, or do not want to leave the place they've grown used to. Due to their struggles they can cause issues for travelers and many travellers choose not to enter this Middle World.

The ones who have departed of their bodies will first find themselves in this place. The spirits of the dead remain here until they leave to go to other realms of existence. So, if someone is suffering from ghosts The Shaman talks to those souls who have died and are responsible for the manifestations within the space. The shamans act as psychopomps to help them find where they are supposed to be.

Because that the Middle World is the one that is the closest to our own and its people are of diverse. Some are compassionate and helpful while others are violent and naughty. You can find helpful spirits in this area and they are the ones that can give the most useful guidance, however you need to be aware of the trickster spirits.

Apart from the specific characters and creatures you can also find energies of thoughts, beliefs as well as intentions and emotions. In the midst of subtle energy, it is possible to see them there too. This will let you discern the energy of objects, people, or even places.

In the mind In the psyche, the Middle World is represented by the conscious mind, or Ego.

III. Upper World

It is true that the Upper World can be thought of as Heaven as well as angels and deities can be found there however it's not quite like it. It's actually the universe and is where the stars reside. It is the home of archetypes and blueprints and possibilities which determine how reality manifests. Anything that is present on the physical world is believed to be an illusion of something that is within the Upper World.

Spirit travelers define this dimension as abstract and mysterious. It is lit through pastel colored light. Beautifully designed temples, castles and other structures can be seen in this area, but it is a an indication of the modern age such as those that are located throughout middle-class areas of Middle World.

There are angels this place, as well as saints, holy persons archetypes, planet beings, and inhabitants of the universe. There are gods that can be seen roaming throughout the world however the ultimate deity is the Creator and the the source of all, is located throughout the Three Worlds.

Although animals are most common throughout their native Lower as well as Middle Worlds, they may be found throughout the Upper World as well but in mythological form. In the higher level of consciousness also known as the superconscious or higher self mind of man is able to find its place in the Word.

Shamans travel to this realm to learn about archetypes, and to guide an idea into being or guide the course of physical events. Interacting with archetypes within this realm allows the Shaman to communicate physically with the people they are. They also visit the realm to gain inspiration and insight on how to restore harmony between the human race, nature and the Divine.

The questions that are typically asked here are not related to worldly, practical issues they are more spiritual and philosophical. It is possible to ask questions about whether a choice is best for the welfare of the people around you or get advice on your purpose in life.

The blueprints of the Universe as well as of life are available, you might be interested in visiting this site for those who want to find out details about the principles of the universe and the secrets of the universe.

Interacting with holy people is best done here.

The remains of the deceased can be seen in this area and this includes pets who have passed away.

How to enter the Upper World

The Upper World could be reached by imagining you're climbing a tree , or a ladder that is reaching the sky. It is also possible to imagine yourself at the top of the world, like a mountain top or a skyscraper. To ascend you can take an elevator or escalator, or imagine yourself being carried up by smoke, a magical carpet or balloon, rocket or even a large bird birds in a flock, or any other thing that rises. You can pretend to be mist or cloud which rises until you reach to the Upper World. You may also be afloat or fly up.

It is possible to enter into the Upper World through a gap between clouds, like the place where sunlight is shining through.

How to travel

Traveling is usually done by lying down and keeping your eyes closed. However, it is also done by sitting, standing in a chair, walking, singing dancing, or chanting. To go beyond your physically Middle World and go to the other realms you have to place yourself in a state of altered of consciousness. This state of mind must be maintained throughout your journey. It is possible to seek out spirits guides to assist you on your journey and assist you in your goal. The journey is made through imagining the trip. Your imagination does not have to be very vivid to be effective.

Find a place that is quiet for 30 minutes to an hour or more. The place you choose should be secure and private. It should also be uncluttered. It is best to have a dark space and you can concentrate on your own thoughts, so it's best to ensure that your eyes aren't distracted by the things surrounding you. It is possible to light incense or candles to can help you relax when you need to.

Make sure you are in the most comfortable position you can find and that doesn't limit your breathing. You can stand, sit or lie down if that's what you like. Breathe in deeply and easily. Close your eyes, or put them in the use of a blindfold or an eye mask. Researcher Michael Harner described a shamanic posture for traveling - lay on your back and stretch your legs. Set your right arm at your side with your fingers spread. Relax your arm, then put it in front of your eyes.

In the event that it aids you to concentrate more, you could be able to sing, chant, or chant. You could play shamanic music, or an audio recording of guided meditation.

Certain have preparation exercises before they begin their shamanic journey. This could take the form of meditative practices such as yoga, breathing exercises (e.g. Pranayama) or other sacred rituals. There is no requirement to practice these, but they can aid in entering more deeply into a Trance.

Concentrate on your goal. It is essential to have a clear intention so that you don't lose yourself on your way. By having a plan, spirits guide you and keep you from getting distracted. Make sure to clearly state your intention within your head. It is also possible to say it in a loud voice. Shamans often chant their intent frequently.

Focus on the sound and the breath (or to the beats of the drum in the case that you are taking note of them). Your body should be instructed to release tension, beginning at the top of your head to your toes. Let relaxation spread to the entire body.

When thoughts begin to invade your mind just let them pass as clouds appear on the edge of the horizon. Don't fight the thoughts as it could cause them to stay longer. Focus on your breathing instead.

It is likely that you will feel stronger sensations as you fall into a state of relaxation. It is possible to feel tingling, and you can hear your ears buzzing. When you're calmed down, you may feel that your heart be faster, and you might notice certain vibrating. Do not be worried about these as they'll soon go away. Be careful not to get too excited, as this can lead to the loss of your the trance.

In this moment, it is possible to be able to see non-physical objects in the vicinity - this could be an indication that you're already on your way. If not, you could see a rope suspended over you. Take a stab at the rope with your spiritual hands (not your hands that are physical) then imagine climbing up it. This will allow you to enter the realm of energy known as The Middle World. You can explore this region or travel to either the Lower as well as the Upper Worlds.

It is recommended that you travel under the guidance of a trusted Shaman. You might want to consider practicing with other people in a group, such as at Shamanic Workshops. If you feel exhausted, suffer from troubling symptoms, experience difficult encounters within the Spirit Realms or feel disengaged from the world and your daily routine, avoid traveling in while until you can find someone to help you.

A Journey Comes to an End

The journeys of the shamanic must come to an be ended at some point. If you're led by drums, you can hear the drumming becoming more intense and louder, or you might hear four distinct beats on the drum. This is called the "callback" and is an indication to get ready to complete your journey. If the callback is heard, speed up with your work. Remind your guides to guide you and say goodbye.

The rhythmic changes could affect your mental state and cause it to return to normal. Your surroundings may change or disintegrate or it could feel like you're getting away from the place.

You can also decide to return, even if you're not hearing drums, or after the callback signal has been heard. Return when you've achieved your goal or when your guides have instructed you to get up or when you are convinced that it is time to end the journey. Tell your guides you must return to normal life.

Let yourself slowly return to your body. It is not necessary to retrace your steps since your consciousness is already in that Middle World and it will be back there by itself. It is just a matter of letting loose your grip on the reality you're in. It is also possible to imagine things that belong to our physical reality, and simply declare within your thoughts that you would like to return now.

As your awareness returns to the physical world Be careful not to be agitated to avoid getting lost or stressing your muscles. Connect to your body. Watch your spirit body merge into your body. Close your eyes gently and slowly. If you see any shining light sources in the area keep your eyes away from them to prevent eye injuries. Relax your body and perform gentle movements with your legs.

If you haven't yet, make a note of every detail you remember during the trip. Do not try to organize or censor your thoughts. The more you write the more likely you'll lose particulars. The objective is to record all you can from your journey. You will be able to sort the information later on a separate sheet in your journal. This way of recording lets you evaluate what transpired, think about the lessons you learned, find answers, and incorporate the lessons you have discovered into your daily routine.

Shamanic Travel Warnings

Shamanic travel can bring positive benefits to your life when you practice it with care and prudence. But, there are risks associated with it.

For example, unrepressed energies are able to come into your consciousness. The traumatizing memories, the hidden emotions and destructive forces could be more easily manifested.

You should be wary of spirits who appear to be useful guides, however are actually evil or malicious entities. The shadow you are among them - it's your self-destructive side and could prevent you from achieving success on your travels.

Genuine spirit helpers won't oblige you to do anything; they will simply advise you on what you should do. They won't force you to commit any act that could be dangerous to you or anyone else.

The process of journeying is best suited to those who are psychologically well-balanced and emotionally and socially well-balanced. Don't go into the process of journeying if you're stressed out because the experiences you have may be an expression of your current state of mind. Keep in mind that on the inner realms, whatever you are thinking about can take on an entirely new life If something unpleasant is bothering you and you are stressed, it could be increased in other realms. This is the primary reason that shamanic travel should be done with the most peaceful mindset that you can.

While it can help with issues, shamanic travel is not the best way to relax and unwind. It can help you access the depths of your being and guidance from the conscious realms. You should be in a good state of mind. If you're exhausted and confused, you'll be more susceptible to the wrath of evil spirits, and you might be lost in self-generated imaginings. The spirits of goodwill may try to aid you but if your head is hazy, you might not be able to hear them clearly.

As we mentioned previously that shamanic travel is not a therapy to relieve stress as it requires access to powerful subconscious sources and communicating with actual conscious beings. There are many other ways to relieve stress that are more secure and more practical

If you're calm and relaxed, you can play shamanic drums to relax your mind.

Grounding

True traditional shamans utilize hallucinogens to help them in their journeys, however they usually live within close contact with the natural world. They are physically and mentally active so their spiritual practices are tempered with their daily life. Contrary to modern-day humans, those living in urban areas are usually disengaged to Mother Nature. People often have minds that are constantly occupied by technology and pursuits of the intellect. Since shamanic travel or other practices could be too stimulating and cause disruption to your daily life and your life, you're more vulnerable to this when you don't live an active life, spend too much time with devices, or work at an office job that requires much thinking.

In this regard, you have to figure out a ways to get grounded and integrate your shamanic experience to your daily life. In addition to keeping you grounded, it allows your life to improve. In the absence of any other help, going to these realms will not bring about any significant changes in your life. After all, shamans visit other realms to receive guidance on how to proceed in the present, and then return to this world to implement their ideas there.

The idea of relying on spirits to help you with your problems is a type of dependence that will stop your improvement and may cause a negative reaction from spirit guides.

Keep in mind that they are watching the actions you take with what they provide. If they see that you're not making use of your shamanic wisdom to benefit others, they may not appear to you anymore. Be aware that you're not an instrument of the spirit realm, but an active co-creator of reality. If you wish to do something, do it no one else will take care of it.

How to ground your Shamanic Journeys

There are ways to bring your shamanic experiences to the reality of your life. One method is sharing your experiences with others particularly those who are knowledgeable about the concept of shamanism and have gone on the journey themselves. You can dress them in physical shape by drawing them, painting them, or creating sculptures of them. To give them a more physical appearance make use of natural materials. For the sake of reflection Write about your experiences. It can be transformed into poems or short stories. You can surround yourself with images or objects that reflect the creatures you encounter.

Real Vs. Imagined

The concept of imagination has always been linked to illusion, but that does not mean that shamanic adventures are only created because they occur in your mind. It is simply the way for your mind to be tuned in to the realities of other dimensions. It is the connection between your mind and the other dimensions. It is possible to imagine things that aren't actually real, but you make them up in a different plane of existence. In is in that plane that they exist but, practically speaking they don't exist in the real world. Although they might be fictional, they could be relevant to you and others who come across them, if they can access the place they are.

There's a distinction between self-created imaginative imagination and non-physical realms. It is important to know the different. If you are able to be in control of what you're seeing or experiencing, it's likely you're making up the scene. If you attempt to imagine a scenario that's distinct from the place you are, and it persists, or if you can alter it, but it returns to the same scene the chances are it to be true. If you are able to master spiritual journeying, you'll be able to create scenes that are consistent.

Shamanic journeys can be challenging for people who are new to the realm of spirits. However, spirits can assist in your travels and other duties. Chapter 5 will discuss useful spirits and how you can find these.

Chapter 11: Work With Plants

Don't consume any psychoactive (mind-altering) plants in case you aren't certain of exactly what's going on. Certain plants can be extremely poisonous even if you use safe plants, you could be killed if you prepare them wrongly or consumed in huge quantities. It is best to use your plants with the supervision of a shaman who has extensive experience with the plants you intend to utilize. There are also people around to assist you in the event that you fall into trouble . For instance, if you are experiencing symptoms that cause anxiety or symptoms, they could offer you an answer, for instance. While many have tried psychoactive substances and have survived however, there are some who did not. Consume these plants at your own risk.

You might have heard accounts of people who've used substances and experienced life-changing, mind-blowing experiences of it. It's true that they occur; many have discovered things they had no idea about and have overcome difficult challenges through the assistance of plant instructors. Most likely, these individuals were warned about the dangers however, their desire to gain knowledge from the spirit of plants won over their fears. Therefore, you must consider: are you willing to endure fear, discomfort and even death, in exchange for the supernatural plant teacher's gifts?

If you're a yes, then it's recommended to make yourself as tough and durable as you can, not just physical, but mentally as well as spiritually. If you suffer from grave psychiatric or medical conditions It is best to stay cautious and refrain from taking psychoactives.

It is important to consult with your doctor and let him/her know about the plans to take the shamanic plant; you could or might not receive the green light based on your health status and the possible reactions of the plant to medications you're taking.

There is no need to take psychoactives in order to enter the realms of spirit and gain access to internal resources, in the end. All you need is to be in an altered state of mind and, as you've learned it is possible to do this in a variety of safe ways.

In that regard the most important aspect of the practice of shamanism is to work with plant spirits. For thousands of years the shamans have been in contact with nature and have discovered which plants are beneficial for humans and which ones are can be harmful. They learned how to prepare them to can achieve the desired results, such as open their mind to undiscovered worlds.

The hallucinogens like psychoactive plants are used for various reasons, including:

* To face their unresolved concerns

* To better understand themselves

* To discover solutions to the most difficult issues

* To gain insight

* To view the world and the people around them in a different manner

* To investigate the other dimensions

* To recognize interactions with spirit as well as subtle energies

People take hallucinogens just to have fun, but being merely interested in the experience could not result in deep insights. Shamans, however, are tolerant of psychoactive plants. They make use of them for important goals that will benefit the entire community.

Shamans have utilized psychoactive plants to work with the spiritual realm and forces. They consume them to enter an alternate dimension where they can accomplish things that are thought impossible in the ordinary world, like communicating to nature spirits, connect with spirits of the deceased, heal illnesses through the energy level and solve problems under the guidance of experienced beings, locate lost objects, discover mysteries, and so on.

As shamans believe that all is alive, conscious as well as intelligent, they see spirits inside plants. For them, they could be healers and teachers while in a state of trance.

Prior to entering trance they are prepared with certain ways to be pleasing to the spirit. The shaman and the participants in their rituals undergo other rituals like drinking ritual baths, and eating a certain diet.

The spirits of plants can appear as humans, animals, or as a mix of both. The way they appear could depend on the circumstances and the person who sees them.

For example The Spirit of Ayahuasca is portrayed as a mother, however it can also appear as snakes. Spirit of Una de Gato Vine manifests its self as a man with claws, however occasionally, it appears as jaguars.

The nature of the plant spirit could differ dependent on the type of feminine or masculine energy is required for healing. For instance one, it is said that the Pucalupuna tree spirit is often seen as a cat-eyed female or at other times, male with multiple heads. But, some spirit animals have a consistent gender. Ayahuasca is believed as female, while Iboga is believed as male.

Sometimes, the appearance of the spirit is linked to the plant's natural. Its name Ayahuma tree is a reference to the spirit head. When the fruit is thrown to the ground, it splits in two. The exposed pulp begins to decay and releases an aroma similar to that of rotting flesh. So, the Ayahuma tree appears as a headless female or a man who has his head inside his chest.

A Sangre of Grado tree's sap that is reddish in color is utilized to treat conditions like wounds, ulcers and infections. The spirit of the tree is believed as one with an red body. The Remocaspi tree is known to appear like a doctor possibly due to its healing properties. The spirits of the tree are said to appear like men of height and power.

Ingestion of psychoactive plant substances is typically performed in an ritual under the guidance of an experienced shaman. The shaman then guides and protect the people in his/her supervision. He/she assists participants in interpreting and process their experiences to integrate them later within their lives.

In order to participate in such an event, participants should be willing to submit to the spirit of the plant. They should not be forced to participate as it's a important matter. Because of the dangers it is only for people who are willing to receiving assistance from the plant spirit regardless of the risk should take part at the event.

Ayahuasca

Ayahuasca is among the most sought-after teachers; its popularity has led to a flurry of tourists to visit Shamans and engage at ayahuasca rituals. Ayahuasca is illegal in nearly all countries , except Peru, Ecuador, Colombia, Bolivia, and Brazil. In these countries there are locations where shamans are able to offer ayahuasca rituals for foreigners.

The Ayahuasca beverage is made up of chacruna and Ayahuasca vine. Both of which are thriving throughout the Amazon rainforest of South America. It is created by the shaman and consumed as a sacred tree in a closed ritual location. It is typically done in the evening in order that participants are able to better see the visions that the drink can trigger.

A week prior to the ceremony, the participants must prepare for the ceremony by following the ayahuasca or dieta. They should avoid processed foods as well as junk food, alcohol and other drugs. Certain diets also prohibit consumption of salt, meat, spices as well as sugar. This is done to prepare your body and mind to be ready for the spirit of plants.

Ayahuasca can cause purging, meaning that participants will vomit and defacate. The toxins are removed from the body and your energy fields. The diet will reduce the intensity of elimination.

The shaman remains in the center, while the others create a circle around him/her. The table with the ayahuasca as well as other shamanic tools are set directly in front of the shaman. Its position in front of participants will help to direct the energy on the spot in which the table lies.

The participants can be seated on mats or chairs. The songs of the Shamanic called Icaros are typically performed to start the ceremony, and to invite positive spirits to join. The Shaman sings in the cup of Ayahuasca, then pours it into the participants' cups. He/she sings in each cup as well.

After everyone has consumed the Ayahuasca tea The candles and lights are shut off. The Icaros is then re-sung along to the rhythms and drums of the Shamanic, and rattles. These sounds help direct energies to cleanse and safeguard the palace. They also help the guests on their journeys and bring the healing they need.

The ceremony can last anywhere from 4 to 6 hours. The effects could begin from 20 minutes up to an half an hour following drinking. It's not advised to drink more simply because the effects aren't yet felt. Drinking too much can make you feel overwhelmed. The effects will be based on the dose of the drink and the components that are used, along with the person's metabolism and the diet.

Participants are not required to ask to drink until the shaman gives the cup. He/she will serve the drink at a specific time when the spirits tell him/her or whenever they believes that the person is at the point of readiness.

When everyone has consumed the cup, they lie in the dark and reflect about what they have experienced. It is best to not talk to one another in order to focus on the messages of the spirit of the plant.

Participants should not leave the sacred space while Ayahuasca is intoxicating. One reason is that the drink can cause confusion as well as the people who drink it feel more sensitive towards the unseeable and attract wandering spirits. If they leave the space, it could expose them to harmful spirits and dangerous energy.

This room is illuminated after the ceremony is over. The shamans and the participants can meet in the moment and discuss about what took place. People who are looking to rest might take a nap.

Food intake is delayed until noon on the following day. Consuming food right after drinking Ayahuasca can cause vomiting.

Ayahuasca is only one of many plants used for healing shamanic practices. Also, be cautious about the substances you consume , and avoid doing things without proper study and planning.

Plant Magic

Shamans utilize plants, not just to heal or for journeying, but they also use them to create magic too. They are distinct from herbalists as they recognize the spiritual and magic applications of plants. There are numerous books on the use of plants to aid in shamanic and magical purposes. The herbs and the methods which are covered will differ in accordance with the tradition.

The belief is that plants can work magic due to the elements that connect all that exists and in specific types that of the plants there exist forces that can be used to achieve particular outcomes like increasing the amount of prosperity, bringing optimism, eliminating negative influences and so on. Utilizing plants with the aim of making their potentials manifest into the world could bring about those outcomes.

Similar to what shamans found Certain plants possess powerful spirits within their midst. They have their own intelligence and can assist people achieve what they wants. When a person is in contact with these spirits, they must be sure they are truly helpful or may make wishes come true in unorthodox ways. The person and spirit must also be able to communicate effectively to avoid miscommunication and erroneous result.

If using plants to create spells, the magician can bless the plants using the energy of the realm of spirit. The energy they use is in harmony with his or her intention. He or she selects the right plants and objects since every item in existence has its own signature of energy which resonates with specific goals and not with others.

Cleaning the Items

Items and plants utilized during the ritual should be cleaned to remove any negative energies which could hinder the magickal process. This is vital when people come in contact with the objects as their energies and thoughts may be entangled to the objects.

Ritual objects can be cleansed by washing it with water, guiding them through smoke from incense and ringing a bell, shaking a rattle around them, or by imagining negative energies being cleansed out of them. You can also seek for the assistance of your guides in spirit and animals to cleanse.

After cleansing, put them in a safe place that is safe for other people to not be able to touch them in order to stop them from infecting the objects by their energies.

Charging

Nature and all things are energy-rich, but you can increase and direct the energy more effectively if you charge the items ahead of casting your spell. After they have been charged then you can use these objects to hold the energy, or let it out to the universe.

The most common methods of charging items include:

* Hold the items using the dominant hand. The hand you use the most frequently is said to release energy more powerfully than the other hand. Imagine your whole body radiant in pure energy. In your mind's eye let the energy flow over the

palms of your hands and be absorbed into your objects.

• Place your items on top of crystals. You can also cover your objects with crystals. Natural crystals have formed over thousands to billions of years and consequently have stored energy. Crystals can be programmed to give energy to your objects. Simply inform the crystals of what they should do. You can also imagine the energy flowing from the crystals into your objects. For the best effect, keep the items surrounded by crystals for the entire day.

* Allow the items to soak up the moonlight. Moonlight is believed by some to be a source of magical energy, whereas sunlight contains more physical energy. Take these objects out prior to sunrise in order to stop it from releasing this subtle energy which is accumulated within the objects.

* Light candles that have a colour that reminds you of your goal For instance, green candles are utilized to heal or bringing clarity and red to ignite passion.

Put your items in a bowl near the candle. Imagine the color and light of the candle dripping into the container in which your objects are.

You can end charging your devices after you have a feeling that they're already full of energy. You may feel an icy breeze, warmth or a tingle when you hold your hand close to the objects. It is also possible to see sparkling sparkles or clear waves that emanate from the objects. Or, you could get the feeling that they're in the process of being ready.

The Ritual

Although rituals that are magical can appear complicated, they're actually symbols of what you wish to occur. The most important thing is to keep your focus on your goals and then visualize the outcome and apply energy to it to allow it to be manifested in the world. There are a variety of magical rituals on the internet and you can experiment with these and develop ones of your own with your shamanic skills. To get the best outcomes, consult your guides in spirit, and do not neglect to act that you can do in your daily life to help you reach your final goal.

Conclusion

You've just discovered the secrets of shamanism that others might not know about. Do you intend to use this knowledge to control other people? Or , would you apply your shamanic wisdom to help improve the lives of other humans? The Spirits are gentle and allow people to choose what they like but they're also willing to allow them to face the consequences of their actions to gain knowledge from it.

Shamanic study cannot be achieved by just reading the pages of a book. Like what was said earlier, it is recommended that you locate a shaman who can teach you about their technique. Spend time with those who have had experience in rituals of shamanism to be able to perform it correctly.

Don't forget that as a shaman your primary teachers are the Spirits. It is important to keep your eyes of shamanism open to their realities However, in the same way you should remain grounded to this reality to ensure that your knowledge will be valuable to the world.

Do not let your education remain at the level of intellectual Perform the exercises, do the tasks. There are people who do not mind studying other people's experiences. It is impossible to be a shaman if you remain at the surface.

Remember that the Spirit loves you. It is eager to bring you positive things and shield your from harm. It is not necessary to be worried about what you'll find in the spirit realms so long as you remain secure within the physical world. Explore to the fullest extent you can and then bring valuable things back. Being an authentic shaman in the present.

www.ingramcontent.com/pod-product-compliance
Lightning Source LLC
Chambersburg PA
CBHW050409120526
44590CB00015B/1891